PRAISE FOR
FINDING YOUR WAY THROUGH CONFLICT

"Amirault and Snyder offer a unique perspective not on resolving conflicts among children, of which much has been written, but on those between the adults who work with them. Drawing on research and experience, they confront an uncomfortable topic with honesty and compassion, combined with practical solutions and encouragement. The authors convincingly argue that you must get into the 'mess' in order to find your way out of it. Then, step-by-step, using a wide range of scenarios, they guide readers through the tangled weeds and sticky swamps toward a clearing of the air. *Finding Your Way Through Conflict* is a timely and valuable manual in an era when conflict, often unrecognized, let alone openly acknowledged, divides us personally and politically, as well as professionally. The book offers readers the work and life skills we all need now. Once learned, and continually relearned, we can pass them on to the next generation."

—**Ann S. Epstein, Ph.D.,** author of *The Intentional Teacher*

"A thank you is in order for Chris and Christine as they offer this vulnerable, insightful, and thought-provoking inquiry into understanding conflict. With decades of early learning expertise and through layering personal encounters that are inherent in the work of serving others, the authors share their own conflicts as well as the toolkit they've developed to assist the reader in handling a range of situations. Far from a one-size-fits-all presentation of magic solutions, this book offers strategies and research that will guide the reader in developing skills for reflection, learning, and improvement. In the words of Chris and Christine, 'If you do not learn these skills, *conflict will erase and silence the very people you seek to serve.*' If you work to serve children and families, you'll want to read this book."

—**Vincent J. Costanza, Ed.D.**, advisor, Bright Start Foundation Advisory Council

"This book is for anyone who wants to feel more confident and capable in handling those keep-you-up-at-night disagreements and simmering resentments. Amirault and Snyder explain the skills, tactics, and mindset you need to turn inevitable conflicts into opportunities for collaboration and growth. Brimming with practical advice and useful insights, this book will not only change how you approach relationships with coworkers, parents, and children, it'll transform how you approach your life."

—**Amy Gallo**, contributing editor at *Harvard Business Review* and author of the *HBR Guide to Dealing with Conflict*

FINDING YOUR WAY THROUGH CONFLICT

Strategies for Early Childhood Educators

Chris Amirault, Ph.D., and Christine M. Snyder, M.A.

Foreword by Ann McClain Terrell

Library of Congress Cataloging-in-Publication Data
Names: Amirault, Chris, author. | Snyder, Christine M., 1981– author.
Title: Finding your way through conflict : strategies for early childhood educators / Chris Amirault and Christine M. Snyder.
Description: Minneapolis : Free Spirit Publishing Inc., 2021. | Includes bibliographical references and index.
Identifiers: LCCN 2020016395 (print) | LCCN 2020016396 (ebook) | ISBN 9781631984945 (paperback) |
      ISBN 9781631984952 (pdf) | ISBN 9781631984969 (epub)
Subjects: LCSH: Early childhood education—Psychological aspects. | Early childhood education—Social aspects. | Conflict
      management—Study and teaching (Early childhood) | Social interaction in children. | Interpersonal conflict in children.
Classification: LCC LB1139.23 .A65 2021 (print) | LCC LB1139.23 (ebook) | DDC 372.21—dc23
LC record available at https://lccn.loc.gov/2020016395
LC ebook record available at https://lccn.loc.gov/2020016396

Edited by Kyra Ostendorf
Cover and interior design by Shannon Porciau

10 9 8 7 6 5 4 3 2 1
Printed in the United States of America

Free Spirit Publishing Inc.
6325 Sandburg Road, Suite 100
Minneapolis, MN 55427-3674
(612) 338-2068
help4kids@freespirit.com
freespirit.com

Free Spirit offers competitive pricing.
Contact edsales@freespirit.com for pricing information on multiple quantity purchases.

To our families, both born and built.

Contents

Foreword

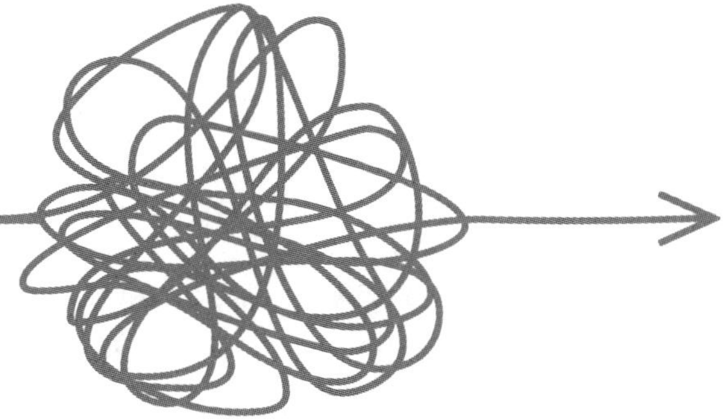

by Ann McClain Terrell

"Peace is not just the absence of conflict; peace is the creation of an environment where all can flourish regardless of race, color, creed, religion, gender, class, caste, or any other social markers of difference."

Nelson Mandela

In *Finding Your Way Through Conflict*, Chris Amirault and Christine Snyder provide those of us in the early childhood education field with guidance and opportunities for reflection and growth in our ability to solve conflicts in the workplace, and, just as importantly, within our own family and community. As the authors point out, we are human and, as such, bring our "stuff" with us into our centers, programs, and classrooms. Our personal and cultural perceptions and assumptions create the lens through which we view conflicts that arise and need to be addressed. Relationships are key to early childhood education, and we must intentionally work to build and sustain meaningful and respectful relationships with each other, our colleagues and coworkers, and the children and families we serve. This deep dive into conflict resolution gives us new knowledge and skills to help us address this issue as we work with our colleagues and serve the children and families in our centers, programs, and classrooms.

Conflict resolution and problem-solving are required of a leader. In my book, *Graceful Leadership in Early Childhood Education*, I describe some real conflict situations that I have faced in my career. One such situation happened at the beginning of my job as the director of a campus-based child care program. About a month in, I had to intervene in a child–parent interaction that occurred during end-of-the-day pickup. I overheard an adult voice coming from the coatroom area. The adult was speaking to a child in a very loud, harsh tone. I approached and observed one of our student parents trying to put a coat on her child. She was also physically hitting the child, and the little girl was crying. I was sure the whole center could hear the interaction, including other parents who were picking up children.

I walked up to the parent and very intently and quietly said to her, "I'm sorry, but I cannot allow you to do that here." The parent looked at me and said in a combative manner something like, "Oh, so you're going to tell me how to raise my child." By now we were being observed by staff members, and I realized that this was an opportunity to model my approach to conflict resolution, as I needed to assess the situation quickly and deliver a response that would address it and meet the parent's and child's needs at the same time. So I responded again by intently and quietly saying to the parent, "My name is Ann Terrell and I am the new director here, and what I'm saying to you is, from one Black woman to another, that if you continue to hit your child, I will have to report you for child abuse." The parent stopped her behavior, looked at me, and said, "No one has ever told me that before." I then stooped down to the child's eye level and, while I helped her put on her coat, said to her that her mother had had a very long day and was probably tired and really needed her cooperation in getting dressed to go home. I walked them to the door, hugged them both, and said I'd see them in the morning. I ended the interaction by saying to the parent that I would be available for her if she ever needed or wanted to talk.

Sometimes conflict resolution can be frustrating when it seems that you're the only one trying to address the perceived problem. During my tenure as director of the campus child care center, we implemented a seven-step approach to problem-solving as part of the curriculum for the children. The preschool rooms served three-, four-, and five-year-old children, and quite often had turnover as the student parents graduated and withdrew their children. There was always a learning curve in our problem-solving approach for the new enrollees. "Francis" started in our program at age two and as the child of faculty, she remained with us to kindergarten entry, so she was very familiar with our approach to problem-solving. Whether it were a conflict at the sensory table or the block area, Francis understood the seven-step approach and implemented it. But one day in the beginning of a new fall semester, a conflict in the preschool classroom arose, as indicated by raised voices. The teacher used the prompt, "We seem to have a problem, can you two tell me what the problem is?" as she approached Francis and another child. The teacher then followed up with, "Francis, there seems to be a problem, how can we solve the problem?" Frances in turn stomped her foot and proclaimed, "I don't want to solve the problem!"

Many of us respond to conflict in this way; we want to hide from and ignore the conflict because we feel we are not adequately prepared to address the situation. Depending on the conflict, sometimes we can dive right in and resolve it. However, sometimes the conflict calls for us to sit with the issue, reflect, and then decide how best to address it. I love the title of this book, *Finding Your Way Through Conflict*. To me, it says that sometimes we must sit with the messiness and be uncomfortable in our reflection on our part in the conflict and how to resolve it.

Skilled conflict-resolution ability provides adults and children the opportunity to be competent and confident in handling these challenging situations, be they with parents, staff, peers, or between children. This book lights the path to finding your way through conflict resolution and to growth in conflict-resolution skills that will carry early childhood professionals throughout our careers.

Best,
Ann McClain Terrell

Introduction

Approaching Conflict

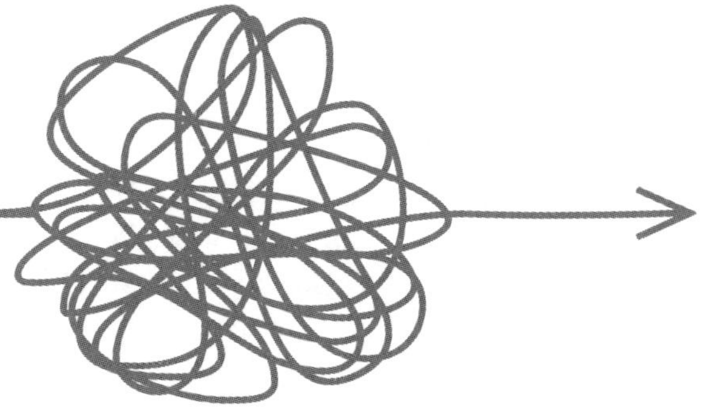

Dealing constructively with tough topics and awkward situations strengthens a relationship. And that's an opportunity too good to pass up.

Douglas Stone, Bruce Patton, and Sheila Heen, *Difficult Conversations*

The teacher who interrupts you whenever you're speaking in meetings and then accuses you of being rude when you point it out. The teammate who smiles while explaining why they chose not to do that unpleasant task, even though they wore that same smile yesterday when telling you that the same task was "No problem." The supervisor who repeatedly reassures you that "You're doing great!" whenever you are in their office but points out flaws every time they walk into your classroom. The veteran colleague who has been glaring at you whenever you pass them in the hallway since you arrived, for who-knows-what reasons.

Read the opening quote again.

These situations are "opportunities"? That are "too good to pass up"?! Yes!

If you take away one insight from this book, make it this: *to learn how to get out of conflict, you must learn how to be in conflict*. And that means turning toward the conflict, inhabiting its nuances fully, and engaging it as a learning opportunity for you, the other person, and the relationship you share. There are no sidelines or shortcuts, no easy ways out. Years of practice with thousands of people in our personal and work lives, along with the research we've gathered here, make it evident that most conflict is just like the famous bear hunt. You can't go over it and you can't go under it. You have to find your way through it.

> To learn how to get out of conflict, you must learn how to be in conflict.

Developing the ability to find your way through conflict requires learning about yourself, others, and behavior change, so you're going to need a healthy dose of patience. You probably picked up this book to get right at those tricky, sticky conflicts—we understand! We share those persistent desires to fix conflicts *right now*. But we've learned that conflict is not quite that simple, and that applying conflict resolution listicles and short-term fixes often does more harm than good.

It can be frustrating to make that time and effort, especially since so many common conflicts seem deceptively simple at first glance. Why can't two colleagues working in the same classroom sort out who's doing what? Surely an instructional coach can find ways to address the problematic practices of a teacher they supervise? And if a parent isn't meeting basic program requirements, it doesn't have to be a confrontation, does it? Sadly, we've learned over and over that such "simple" conflicts are complex, nuanced situations that require careful thinking and reflection. After all, if they are so simple, why do they keep happening?

Following years of workshops with thousands of participants, we are certain that you can learn effective strategies that take into account the complexity and nuances of conflict. Indeed, throughout the book, we refer to how each of us has built up our tolerance for conflict, learning and using the skills we now have in our toolbelts and will share with you. Along with tales of success, we also share our stories of self-discovery as we confront new challenges from within new conflicts, a process that is ongoing for us both.

Making the decision to confront conflict from within it is the most challenging, important shift in perspective that effective conflict engagement requires, a shift we hope you'll enact throughout the book. But don't despair. We are confident that you—yes, you—can make that shift and learn how to be in and get out of conflict. Welcome to the bear hunt!

Conflict in Early Childhood Education

This book focuses on the world of conflicts faced in the work of early childhood education. And while we will at times refer to conflicts with children and with families, this book engages primarily with conflicts involving early childhood colleagues. Here's why.

When the two of us first met several years ago, we were both well into our careers in the early childhood profession. Christine had been devoting a great deal of time to thinking about how classrooms could best support young children's social and emotional development. Chris had been working with early childhood teachers and administrators on how best to nurture diversity and promote equity for the children and families they serve.

But when we sat down to talk about our work, our shared attention shifted to adult conflict in the field. Christine kept noticing that the adult teachers, more so than the young children, were the ones having difficulty working through and recovering from squabbles. Chris reflected that people's natural discomfort with negotiating differences could make already fraught topics of ethnicity, race, sexuality, and so on far more challenging.

As it turns out, our conversation is one of many conversations on conflict that have been occurring across the profession. Throughout the book, we show how adult conflict in early childhood education is at the center of much of the classroom quality research and metrics that are reshaping our understanding of children's learning environments and the relationships that support them. Concepts such as attunement, co-regulation, primary and secondary trauma, and teacher self-efficacy have become important perspectives that early childhood educators can use to rethink how they engage with conflict in their work.

We have broadened our two-way conversation into a dynamic active-learning experience through presentations on conflict at national early childhood conferences, and we hope this book contributes to the growing discourse that we feel is vital to our profession. The hundreds of amazing early childhood educators we have met in our careers are people who can tackle the thorniest child developmental issues with confidence, rigor, and ease. But if you put many of those same people into a conflict with a peer, they hesitate to engage with the conflict, they avoid the work the conflict produces, and they become uncomfortable and awkward. Adult conflict can shatter the self-efficacy of some of the best early childhood teachers in a heartbeat.

Finally, though there are workplace conflicts in early childhood education settings that involve multiple people, most conflicts unfold and should be addressed within one-on-one relationships. To understand the dynamics within one-on-one conflict, this book focuses on two specific individuals: you and your counterpart. We are confident that learning about these two folks will aid you in every conflict, large or small!

The important work of supporting young children's learning and growth can also support your own learning and growth in conflict. Learning how to work through conflict starts with understanding some core principles.

> Conflict is a natural part of life, a normal component of social interaction that activates our deepest humanity.

The Six Core Principles of Working Through Conflict

Over the years, we've found ourselves repeating these to ourselves and to others, as they often reveal important perspectives we're missing when conflicts arise. We return to these core principles throughout the book, illustrating their value in even the trickiest conflicts. See also page 81 for a one-page reproducible of the principles.

Conflict Is Natural, Normal, and Deeply Human

This principle, in a calm moment of reading, may appear completely obvious: conflict is a natural part of life, a normal component of social interaction that activates our deepest humanity. Of course, we don't feel that way when we are in conflict. Instead, we feel misunderstood. Everything is off kilter; our usual selves and skills have vanished, replaced by a clunky, demanding set of thoughts and feelings that do not reflect who we really are. But those feelings are precisely what connect us to the rest of humanity. Recognizing this commonality can help us have greater empathy for others—and ourselves— in the midst of conflict.

Conflict Is the Work, Not a Distraction from the Work

Nearly everyone who has attended our workshops over the years describes conflict as the thing that prevents them from doing their real work. We believe conflict *is* the work. But, as far as we are aware, few if any higher education programs, early childhood agencies, and professional development systems teach adult conflict as a core component of that work. So, instead of seeing conflict as an impediment or distraction, we place it front and center as the work itself—and, we're convinced, usually the most important work.

Conflict Is Almost Always Reciprocal

Conflicts typically drive us into a defensive posture. That's how the blame game begins: as we experience the problems created in the conflict, we extend our index finger to point out that their source exists elsewhere. Unfortunately for our egos, it's rarely that simple. In our experience, the majority of conflicts are reciprocal, which means that everyone contributes their fair share—even though they're usually well-meaning individuals trying to do what's right in tricky situations. To help you see your part of conflict, there are sections of the book where we prompt you to fess up to your role in the mess. And it turns out this is a very effective conflict resolution strategy all by itself.

Conflict Exists If Someone Says It Does

Routinely, the conflicts that have been brought to our attention seem one-sided, at least to one of the parties. In those situations, while the aggrieved person is feeling troubled, offended, disrespected, or worse, the other person doesn't even see the problem. So following from the last principle, we assert that, if one person declares a given situation is a conflict, then there's a conflict. The collaborative relationships between adults that drive most early childhood workplaces simply cannot function properly if one person is ignoring another person's concerns. So, if someone calls foul, it's time for both parties to make a good-faith effort to work it out.

Conflict Is Sustained by Win/Lose, Right/Wrong Thinking

Skillfully negotiating conflict is never just yes or no, easy or hard. In fact, conflict feeds off of that sort of either/or thinking; it's the gasoline that makes the engine run—and often splashes out of the tank, where a spark can set the car on fire! So to learn how best to negotiate conflict, you'll need to learn how to live in the middle—in the ambiguous zone—and that is a real challenge for most of us. Our families, our cultures, our educations, even our neurology: they all drive us into this sort of either/or thinking, so we teach you in this book how to resist it by developing a thorough understanding of how to avoid either/or perspectives as often as possible.

Conflict Never Stops Teaching Us

Finally, we encourage you to approach the work of this book with humility and respect for the endlessly fascinating world of conflict. In our workshops, we always share a humorous anecdote about a conflict that the two of us have had recently—often with each other. We do that because we are convinced that no one ever stops being in or learning about conflict. We hope that you'll join us with a similar sense of humor and curiosity, recognizing that every conflict is a fascinating study of people, particularly ourselves, that includes new insights and nuances worth exploring. Not only will this attitude help you establish a bit of distance from which to perceive individual conflicts, but you can also develop new perspectives and skills within those conflicts as a result. The only way to solve any given conflict is to study it from within.

How This Book Is Organized

The chapters ahead are organized around the following set of components. Each chapter focuses on key concepts that are central to understanding conflict. We take time to explain those concepts in detail, and we delve into the research insights that enrich our understanding of them. We explore why they matter, demonstrating how the key concepts arise in the real world of conflict. In those sections we also provide appropriate, real-world examples, situations that we dissect using the concepts we've just presented.

Finally, each chapter describes precisely what to do and how to do it. We want you to develop agency and confidence in conflict, and that requires two things: a set of tools, concrete actions, reflective exercises, and practical steps to take within conflict, and a set of critical stances, attitudes and perspectives that are necessary to cultivate in order to use the tools effectively.

How to Use This Book

Before we dive in: if you've picked up this book because you are deep within a complex, urgent conflict, we want to add a note of support and guidance. We also want to encourage you to approach all conflicts with patience and self-awareness. This approach is especially critical when situations feel urgent; as we discuss in chapter 3, that urgency can prevent your brain from doing what you need to do to find your way through the conflict.

We are fully aware that you may want to skip ahead to check out later chapters that lay out steps for conflict engagement right now. So we've built the book to include the patience

All conflict engagement with others must start with an inventory of what you will be bringing into that conflict yourself.

and self-awareness in those steps. Chapter 5, in particular, makes it clear that all conflict engagement with others must start with an inventory of what you will be bringing into that conflict yourself.

We are sure that you truly will benefit from the seeming delay created by sorting out the emotions you do and don't bring into your conflicts. Exploring those emotions can be tricky, so we strongly recommend that you do the reflective exercises when you are on relatively solid personal and professional ground, and that you have a close friend, partner, or colleague available to support you.

The support can be strengthened with someone who is also reading this book, as together you will gain skills for finding your way through conflict. And if you're able to work with colleagues, the exercises in chapter 2 are excellent for developing conflict skills in teams. We've found that this sort of shared self-reflection is invaluable for everyone working in an early childhood setting. Whether you're reading alone or in a group, be sure to download the professional learning community (PLC) guide we wrote to accompany the book. It's a useful resource on ways to share in the learning and has additional information we think you'll enjoy. It can be downloaded at freespirit.com/PLC.

Additionally, this book focuses on both a reflective process and an in-the-moment-of-conflict process in which we reference some useful foundational content that is typically initiated in the development of a program and discussed in new-hire orientation. This foundational content includes program mission statements, job descriptions, and field standards like the National Association for the Education of Young Children (NAEYC) Code of Ethical Conduct, to name a few. We've provided guidance for use of these tools in relation to conflict situations in chapter 6, but if you find yourself in the beginning stages of developing this foundational content, we encourage you to utilize the activities in the PLC as well as outside resources focused on developing a new program or new teams. NAEYC, Head Start, and local and state early childhood resource entities can be useful places to start.

This is a book that we hope you'll read and reflect on, and then come back to as new conflicts arise. Whether you are reading on your own or with your team, we are so glad to have you with us on this journey into conflict. Let's get started!

CHAPTER 1

DEFINING CONFLICT

As we welcome you on your journey into and out of conflict, let's focus on what may seem like an obvious question: what, exactly, do we mean by *conflict*? Like many abstract concepts, *conflict* is a term we use while assuming that others know what we mean. Unfortunately, most of us fail to define the term, both to ourselves and to others. In the midst of a situation that's tricky enough, we're operating without clear individual or shared definitions.

As a result, defining conflict is an important part of finding the way through it. The definition helps us understand how we're approaching the situation, what we value and prioritize, and it can do the same for the person with whom we are struggling. But it's not easy.

Quite regularly, a teacher or administrator will ask us in a hushed tone of voice, "Do you have to call this a 'conflict' workshop? I mean, 'conflict' sounds . . . so harsh!" Instead of providing some reassuring insights about working through conflict, people sometimes suggest that our use of the very word *conflict* produces it.

> Defining conflict is an important part of finding the way through it. The definition helps us understand how we're approaching the situation, what we value and prioritize.

Every time we've attempted to refine our definition of conflict over the years, we've learned more about the complex set of cultural, organizational, and personal subtleties that each person brings to the work of conflict engagement and resolution. So with humility about the task ahead, we devote this chapter to defining conflict.

As with any conflict, the devil is in the details, and throughout the book, we encourage you to pause and write down some specifics concerning one or two conflicts in which you're currently embroiled. Doing so will help you see how you decide what is and what is not a conflict, decisions that will help you flesh out your own definition.

Of course, it's impossible for us to know about your specific conflicts. So, in the next section, we introduce five scenarios that typify many of the sorts of conflicts we've heard from our colleagues over the years. As we explore these situations and perspectives on what is a conflict and why, it's likely that your definition of conflict will evolve. Keep in mind that the goal of defining conflict is not for everyone to have identical definitions. Rather, the goal is for each of us to develop a better understanding of our own definition of conflict, to recognize that other people have different definitions, and to consider the deep underlying components that contribute to our reactions to conflict.

Five Conflict Scenarios

For each of the following scenarios, jot down some notes and consider three things:

- Is this a conflict? Why or why not?

- If this is a conflict, what exactly is the issue producing the conflict?

- How comfortable are you engaging in this conflict? Are you likely to dive right in or run in the other direction?

Scenario One

You are pulling into the parking lot at work, and there is a car leaving. The driver is a parent from another classroom. They roll down their window and begin berating you for a political bumper sticker on your car. *Is this a conflict?*

If this is a conflict: What exactly is the conflict here? The driver berating you? Your political bumper sticker? The driver's presumption that it's okay to berate you?

Scenario Two

You're a preschool teacher. You recently put up some new child-centered artwork in your classroom. One morning, you notice that your co-teacher has removed it without asking you. *Is this a conflict?*

If this is a conflict: What exactly is the conflict here? The artwork being taken down? Your co-teacher not asking you? Your lack of trust in your co-teacher's decision-making—or their lack of trust in yours?

Scenario Three

You are a toddler teacher. One of the new children in your classroom was recently adopted and enrolled in your program immediately afterward. After seeming to have adjusted well for the first two weeks, the child bursts into an inconsolable tantrum for no apparent reason. *Is this a conflict?*

If this is a conflict: What exactly is the conflict here? The child's tantrum? Your inability to understand the cause of the tantrum?

Scenario Four

You are a director of family services. An employee bursts into your office and angrily confronts you. They insist that you discriminated against them in the staff meeting the night before, which is shocking to you. *Is this a conflict?*

If this is a conflict: What exactly is the conflict here? The employee's angry disruption? Their allegations of discrimination? Your discriminatory actions?

Scenario Five

You are an instructional coach. One of your first-grade teachers has a student who repeatedly ignores the teacher's classroom instructions. As you observe, the child again ignores the activity the teacher is scaffolding, and you watch the teacher perform the activity for the child. *Is this a conflict?*

If this is a conflict: What exactly is the conflict here? The child's refusal to comply with the teacher? The teacher completing the task for the child? Your choice not to step in to give feedback to the teacher?

Now take a look at what you've written for all five scenarios and, if you considered the scenario to be a conflict, reflect on how comfortable you are engaging in it. Take a moment to rate each scenario in this way. Are you likely to dive right in or run in the other direction? This reflection will help you begin an exploration of what sorts of conflicts are most challenging for you. The conflicts we are worst at engaging are the ones we want to avoid the most.

Keep your notes handy as you determine your own definition of conflict.

Defining Conflict

Here are a few informal definitions of conflict we've heard in our work, some of which may resonate for you:

"When two people disagree about something important."

"An unresolved, heated argument."

"A problem between two people or groups of people who can't get along."

"A serious, long-term dispute."

"A dilemma that escalates to the point of mistreatment."

"Whatever is happening with this other person, it's not about me."

Which of these informal definitions best describes your understanding of conflict? We're going to unpack those definitions and dig below the surface of each one. We also return to the five scenarios above and share some of the responses we've gotten over the years. Finally, we continue to ask you to generate and mull over some conflicts of your own. As you do, we think you'll learn a lot about conflict—and a lot about yourself.

Conflict in Organizations

Conflicts in early childhood settings differ from those in our personal lives with friends, family, and acquaintances for a variety of reasons. Most importantly, workplace conflict comes with its own organization-specific nuances in the form of rules and expectations, whether stated clearly or not. Let's start with those basics.

> **Workplace conflict comes with its own organization-specific nuances in the form of rules and expectations.**

If you are having conflicts at work, we urge you immediately to find the documents that your organization uses to define workplace interactions: job descriptions, employee handbooks, grievance procedures, family or client guidelines, and so on. If these don't exist in your workplace, now is a great time to start a conversation. It's essential that you understand how your organization describes conflict and the processes used to engage and resolve it, and you should seek out all available human resources (HR) personnel and documentation if you're lucky enough to have them.

At the very least, you need to know the processes that exist for your protection as you make your way through workplace conflict. If they exist, your organization's HR materials will help you define some of the critical concepts that you'll need should your situation escalate from a workable interpersonal dilemma into a crisis that threatens your well-being or employment. In addition, conflicts involving workplace harassment or discrimination have state and federal laws that require very specific attention. Finally, supervisors and other HR professionals can be vital resources, often trained to help you navigate any significant workplace conflict.

As you peruse your organizational definitions and processes, you are likely to find that the workplace they describe on paper and the one to which you report every day are very different. That's because workplaces aren't merely a collection of explicit, intentional actions described in written texts. Like all collections of human beings, workplaces are a constantly evolving network of collaborative relationships that, together, make a culture.

That is to say: while these documents are critical to your position within an organization and can be essential in conflict situations, no employee handbook or grievance procedure captures any real-world workplace culture in all of its complexity. Yet conflicts are submerged in that cultural complexity.

Conflict in Culture

You've probably seen a version of the familiar iceberg diagram. Here's our take on it.

There are many cultures to which we belong and in which our relationships to our work and each other have shared meaning and value. All communication is always situated within those fluctuating meanings, relationships, and values; even though the words stay the same, the iceberg is always shrinking, growing, and shifting under the surface.

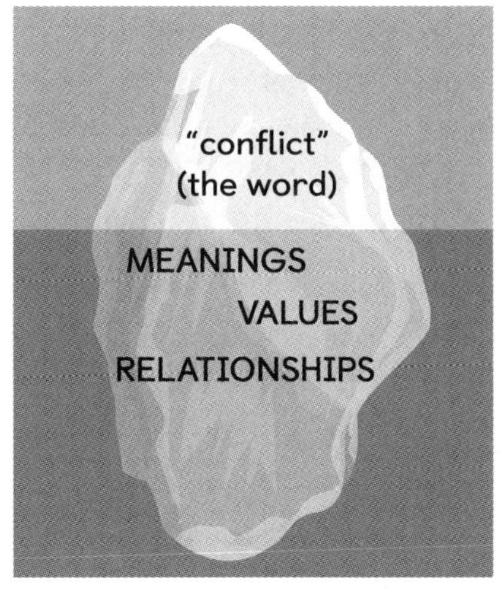

But we often forget this insight when we're in conflict and, instead, cling to our own understanding as if it's definitive. In addition, we often use words as if their meanings, relationships, and values are shared by others. We assume that other people are above the surface of the water with us.

And that's a big problem. Have you ever noticed that, when you're stuck in a conflict, words can suddenly fall apart, revealing that you and someone else don't share an understanding of a situation, person, or expectation that you thought you shared? Without trying, you can find yourself in a big mess: suddenly, someone with whom you thought you had a good working relationship sounds like a person whose values oppose your own.

We have found that the organizations that ask for our help with conflict often have not clarified those critical meanings, values, and relationships. As a result, we want to stress the importance of devoting time and effort to that process for any organization that wants to build conflict resolution skills. We're convinced that, in organizations that don't do this work, workplace culture contributes to the conflict through its very silence.

Organizations often focus their efforts on naming their positive components, such as shared values about collaboration, positive intent, and shared understanding. Unfortunately, simply naming something doesn't actually translate to the doing of it. A focus on the positive often means the organization is actively avoiding the flip side. Given that we're all imperfect human beings, it's inevitable that we'll find it challenging to collaborate with some colleagues, deciding that they are the problem and refusing to see things from their perspective. When organizations are silent about this work, our inability to live up to organizational ideals can feel like a personal failure; to an individual struggling with a conflict, that organizational silence can feel like a whispered critique.

Defining conflict requires that we break organizational silence, at both the policy and personal levels. After all, the cultures of the organizations for which we work are a stew of all of the individual culture aspects we bring to our professional lives—regional, familial, spiritual, ethnic . . . you name it. We need to feel supported in our exploration of the diverse cultural nuances each of us bring to work. If we don't feel supported, we're likely to shut down, protecting ourselves and keeping our meanings, values, and relationships below the surface. In doing so, we amplify the tension and murkiness of conflict.

Five Big Questions

In any conflict situation, it's useful to ask yourself the following questions. Pay special attention to the italicized terms, most of which come from some of the informal definitions at the start of the chapter:

- Do you and the other person feel the situation is equally *important* and *serious*?

- Does one of you think the situation is *unresolved* while the other person feels it is *resolved*?

- Do your exchanges feel *safe* for one person but *heated* for another person who feels *mistreated*?

- Does one person think this situation just popped up while the other person feels it's a *long-term* mess that's now *escalating*?

- Is one of you complaining that you *can't get along* while the other is thinking, "It's *not about me*"?

Think about a conflict you're in right now, or speculate about what it would be like to be in one of the scenarios described earlier.

Which of the above questions feel particularly potent?

Which ones are tricky to answer?

Which ones feel irrelevant—and is it possible that the question is irrelevant for you but very relevant for the other person?

Finally, did you notice that aspects of the conflict that initially seemed straightforward became more and more complicated as you pondered these questions?

Welcome to being *in* conflict. We realize that, like most people, you probably want to get to the business of pinpointing the conflict to start resolving it. But, alas, we have learned the hard way that navigating these questions—and the icebergs that may be submerged beneath them—is the essential first step.

If you want to resolve conflicts, your personal dictionary needs your definitions not just for the term *conflict* but for several others.

- How do you define *importance*?

- When is an exchange *serious* for you, and when is it *heated*?

- What are your criteria to determine whether a situation is *resolved*?

And your dictionary isn't enough: you need access to your counterpart-in-conflict's dictionary as well.

In a perfect world, it would be wonderful if you could have a friendly chat with your counterpart, make a long list of key terms, and agree enthusiastically on a set of shared definitions. Conflicts rarely allow for such reasonable discussions at the start. So here we offer you two fundamental steps toward definition, both of which are strong foundations for successful conflict resolution.

The first is listening carefully for what someone else feels is important. Are they referring to "respect"? Does the situation feel "out of synch" to them? It requires you not to focus on what *you* think is serious and important but to listen for their use of those same words.

The second step is to ask a seemingly basic question: "What do you mean by _____?" This is trickier than it sounds. It requires empathy (not defensiveness), logical engagement (not emotional reactivity), and authenticity (not fake-nice "interest"). These are the three components of trust as outlined by Frances Frei in her terrific TED Talk on the subject. And they are the reasons why it's so powerful to ask, "What do you mean?": you're taking an empathetic, logical, authentic step into the conflict, and therefore beginning to build a way out.

When you ask, "What do you mean by _____?" with sincerity, the answers will allow you to dive into someone else's cultural ocean. You'll gain a glimpse of the meanings and values that are part of that person's understanding—meanings and values that this conflict has revealed and that are important to the person with whom you want to sort it out. What's more, you'll have a chance to articulate your own meanings and values in response, initiating a dialogue that will come as a small but meaningful relief in most situations. There's no right or wrong here, either, which allows you to take on a broader perspective regarding a situation that feels stuck.

You in Conflict

When we first started doing this work on conflict, we relentlessly emphasized the importance of seeing things from the perspective of the person with whom you are engaged in conflict. That perspective-taking remains essential. But over the years, we realized that we were rushing through another essential step, and perpetuating a key problem at the root of every conflict: knowing the "you" who is in the conflict you're in.

One of our favorite sayings about conflict comes from Poland, and it translates roughly as "Not my circus, not my monkeys." As early childhood educators we tend to step into circuses that aren't ours and try to wrangle monkeys that are not our responsibility. We are fixers of problems and righters of wrongs, and thus we often benefit from this helpful reminder to keep our boundaries distinct and strong.

There's only one problem with this sage advice: it doesn't work with conflict. Any conflict that you are in is, by definition, your conflict. That means it's your circus, and you are one of the monkeys. Sorry!

Put differently, you are one of the contributors to the conflict, even if your only contribution is your response (or lack thereof) to someone else's actions. After all, if you're in a conflict, that means that the boundaries of the conflict enclose you—that's literally what "in a conflict" means.

We emphasize this obvious point to offset the typical human response to conflict: "C'mon, this is about them; it's not about me." But, if you are in a conflict, we guarantee that you bring all of "you" into it, especially the irrational, illogical, and muddled parts.

As a result, in conflict you engage parts of yourself that you know and recognize, but you also bring other parts that you probably don't know and recognize quite as well. This can be challenging, for few of us like to admit our shortcomings. As you activate your intelligence and clear thinking, you also bring your irrational reactions, defensiveness, and messy feelings. You use straightforward words that float above the surface of the water, and those words inevitably point to murkier values, meanings, and relationships that are submerged.

> In conflict you engage parts of yourself that you know and recognize, but you also bring other parts that you probably don't know and recognize quite as well.

This stew of awareness and confusion, of insight and ignorance, needs patient attention if you want to get good at conflict. Consider the following questions to further develop your understanding of the "you" you bring to conflict:

- What experiences have tended to produce conflicts for you at work? At home? In your community?

- When you're in a conflict, what meanings, values, and relationships feel most important or most at risk?

- When you refer to those meanings, values, and relationships with words like *respect*, *understand*, and so on, what exactly do you mean by those words?

- When you have resolved a conflict with someone, what has been resolved?

Reflecting on these questions helps to emphasize the rational, logical perspectives that you bring to conflict. Consider the definitions you hold and the assumptions you make in tricky situations. These cognitive exercises are critical to building your conflict resolution tool kit, and we urge you to take that homework seriously.

But that homework is not enough. When you are in conflict, you're not just using your cognitive skill set. Conflict is an emotional, bodily experience. You feel scared or angry, miffed or outraged. Your speech pace and volume increase or decrease; your shoulders and jaw tighten. You turn your gaze away or close your eyes; you sweat; you stammer; you hold your breath.

So we encourage you to revise your homework by reframing each question to emphasize those emotions and sensations.

- What does it feel like, emotionally and physically, when you are in conflicts at work? At home? In your community?

- What meanings, values, and relationships make you nervous, angry, or scared?

- When you have resolved a conflict, how does your body respond, and what emotions do you feel—and stop feeling?

Both of us have learned the dangers of prioritizing our thinking in conflict and ignoring our sensations and emotions. Logic is important; don't get us wrong. But logic can also be a way to avoid the other parts of ourselves that we bring into conflict. Whether we like it or not, our messy, unpleasant feelings are always, always part of our conflicts.

All of You in Conflict

In this section, we propose a brief but powerful exercise that provides insight into your emotional contributions to conflict. This exercise draws from a number of different sources, but the primary one we reference is the practice of reflective supervision, a technique that encourages supervisors of human service workers to talk openly and frankly with supervisees about their work. One important component of reflective supervision involves exploring how deep-seated feelings and desires show up in the work that we do.

In a reflective supervision discussion with an early childhood educator, a supervisor will not only talk with us about the details of a given situation with a child or family member, but they will also explore the ways in which our complex feelings, desires, and intentions help or hinder our work in that situation. The supervisor facilitates that exploration, prompting the investigation of complex meanings, emotions, and experiences and providing support and information that helps the supervisee answer their own questions. This exploration is especially important for early childhood educators who are expected to do the very same things for the children and families they serve.

In this way, reflective supervision activates *parallel process*. Reflective supervision sessions are intended to focus on the ways that certain relationships impact other relationships. In that sense, the process creates parallels, finding alignments between the supervisor/supervisee relationship and the teacher/student relationship, for example.

When we looked at teachers who were interacting with noncompliant children, for example, we saw parallels to the ways that those teachers interacted with colleagues, supervisors, and parents. Teachers who avoided angry children also avoided angry parents; teachers who ignored tearful children seemed to take distance from colleagues struggling with grief.

We now know that these parallels in our responses to conflict have significant corroboration in current research on co-regulation. Co-regulation is a complex but essential pattern of interactions that, over time, establishes self-regulation and the ability to manage thoughts, actions, and emotions. Co-regulation is a key component in secure, healthy adult-child relationships (Rosanbalm and Murray 2017). Adults with a healthy sense of their own self-efficacy co-regulate to develop the self-efficacy of children.

The reverse is also true: dysregulated adults have a negative impact on children's social, emotional, and behavioral development. This research is still developing, but we are convinced that the toxic environment adults create for children has a negative impact on the ways children interact with each other and manage their own emotions (Murray, Rosanbalm, and Christopolous 2016). And that means that your ability to manage your own responses to situations at work is a critical component of the environments you create and the relationships that support and sustain those environments.

The following exercise uses the tools of reflective supervision to help you sort out some of those responses. In particular, it will help you identify the feelings that can cause you to slip into dysregulation while at work. Take a piece of paper and write the following words on the page:

Sadness   Anger   Disappointment   Frustration   Shame   Fear

Now take a few moments to reflect on the last two or three difficult situations you've found yourself in at work: frustrating parents, dysregulated preschoolers, challenging colleagues. As you reflect on those situations, try to identify what you were feeling in each moment.

With that reflection in mind, put a check mark on each emotion that you experienced comfortably and safely during those situations. We're not asking for you to say you *like* the emotion; we are finding out whether you can, in the normal course of your day and life, feel a sense of acceptance when you're experiencing it. If you have additional emotions to include, write those too. Even positive emotions like excitement and joy are helpful to note.

Chris has been thinking about this a lot.

I've been in education for my entire professional life, and one of my proudest regular accomplishments is watching someone I've mentored take the next step in their career. Last week, it happened to two of my favorite lead teachers, both of whom have become master teacher/coaches at a different school in my agency. Watching them transition onto a new leadership team with grace and intelligence, I can feel a sense of sad nostalgia about working together for years to reach this moment.

But the sadness doesn't feel awkward or unsafe. Instead, the sadness feels right, like a moment of passage for someone at this stage of my career, something I can observe in myself without feeling thrown off. In fact, I kind of like the sadness, thinking about the wonders of watching people you value and admire grow into leaders.

Sounds entirely okay, doesn't it? That's what you should be looking for, the emotions that feel okay even if they aren't "positive."

Have you checked off those comfy emotions? Great! Now comes the trickier part.

Take a look at the remaining emotions, and circle the ones that are uncomfortable for you to experience, the ones that can take away your sense of safety. These are the ones that make you think "Uh oh" when you sense them in your body—if you're even able to think about them at all.

Unfortunately for Christine, she recently struggled with an emotion that's most difficult for her.

I recently started a new job as the center director of a program with 38 full-time teaching staff and approximately 150 children. It's hard work, and I have had to face a lot of unexpected challenges working with new staff, children, and families in a new environment. But recently I faced a challenge that didn't come from without; the challenge came from within.

During a peak time in flu season, there were several days in a row when a dozen teachers or more were out of the building either sick or supporting sick loved ones. This created many complex staffing challenges in almost every classroom in my building. Staffing is tight in most early childhood centers even on a good day so this situation would be difficult for any program to navigate! But the logistics weren't really the issue for me.

Instead, even though I knew that forces outside of my control were creating the challenges, I felt a powerful sense that I was letting others down. Even though flu season happens every year and I certainly cannot change that, and we worked together to create the best staffing plan possible with the resources we had, I felt a deep responsibility for helping the teachers who were able to get to work endure the challenging week.

This sense of responsibility translated quickly into shame and self-doubt. While I was able to show up each day with a plan, a positive game face, and genuine acknowledgment of the teachers' efforts, as the week wore on the cloak of shame became heavy on my shoulders.

To be sure, most early childhood program leaders would feel a sense of responsibility in a situation like this. But I'm convinced that my dysregulation was more intense due to my relationship to that shame. I woke up frequently at night covered in sweat; I cried on the drive home from work (which I never do); I caught myself stress-eating sugary foods. Most horribly, I had great difficulty connecting with the people I trust the most.

So we encourage you to follow courageous Christine. Identify those emotions that throw you into dysregulation.

Now there's one last step.

Big Feelings and Co-regulation

Once again, reflect on those tricky situations from the last week or so, in particular your interactions with the children in your care, and look at each of the emotions in the list. This time draw squares around the emotions that make you most uncomfortable when other people, especially children, exhibit them. And if you have some emotions both circled and squared, that's okay.

These emotions with squares around them are likely the ones that make you step away from a child to "give her space," the ones that make you say, "You're okay!" when a child clearly isn't. We serve children best when we can connect to them and affirm all of their feelings. So which are the feelings that you find trickiest to affirm with compassion and intimacy?

> **We serve children best when we can connect to them and affirm all of their feelings.**

For Chris, sadness is definitely not one of those feelings. He's got a pretty resilient ability to connect to children who are in tears about a bumpy drop-off or a missed turn. Meanwhile, given Christine's difficulty to process and accept her own feelings of shame, she's likely to feel the same challenge with others. When children exhibit difficulty with shame, her brain immediately tells her to flee: "This is getting too hard!"

We bring up these important emotions because they are crucial to finding your way through conflict, which routinely involves every single one of those emotions. A conflict might make you feel many uncomfortable emotions at the outset—anger, disappointment, fear, frustration, and shame are at the top of our personal lists. People often rush through conflict to avoid those feelings, not because the person or conflict is itself a threat but because experiencing those feelings is simply too difficult. When a conflict brings up those risky emotions in you or in someone else, you might feel completely thrown.

Recognizing the impact those difficult feelings have on us is vital to understanding who we each are in our conflicts with adults—and, as you have probably suspected, in conflicts with young children too. Look carefully at any emotions you've circled twice. Interactions that promote a child's healthy emotional development necessarily include every emotion, even the ones you really don't like.

Through co-regulation, children imitate our responses and reactions to emotions. There are two ways we can support children in this process of social and emotional development. First, if we want children to express and manage their emotions, we as adults need to model managing our emotions, especially when they feel big or uncomfortable. Second, the way we talk to children becomes the way they think about themselves and engage in self-talk.

Therefore, it is essential that we respond to children's outsized emotions with patience and understanding so that, when they feel big things, they understand that difficult feelings are normal and temporary. If we aren't able to respond to and support the range of emotions, even the ones that make us feel most uncomfortable, that carries over to the children we care for, and they will struggle to manage their own emotions too.

Reflect On the "You" in Conflict

Both of us have used exercises like this to explore our own tendencies in conflict and to support others in their reflections. As a result, we have become quite expert in connecting angry, frustrated adults and raging, mid-tantrum children.

Engaging in this kind of reflection and developing humble self-awareness hasn't been easy, and it won't be easy for you either. Having said that, we have genuine hope—and we want you to be hopeful too. Remember that our entire early childhood education field is based on the presumption that humans can change and grow. We know that generational effects aren't fate. We know that both biological and non-biological caregivers can nurture, organize, and even delight in the emotions children experience.

With self-reflection, our approach to conflicts can change and grow too, allowing us to find our way through conflict. As you reflect on your experience with this exercise, start with some basic questions.

What does it evoke in you?

What aspects of your own experience feel particularly resonant? Difficult? Important?

Now think about your current sense of comfort regarding the emotions you circled or squared.

How do those emotions inhabit your body?

Does the fear hunch your shoulders?

Does the anger clench your fists?

And, most importantly for this book: *When does conflict activate your sense of insecurity and risk? With whom? When? How?*

As you develop a sense of this difficult emotional terrain, you will learn how to define conflict and its threats. Of course, your recognition alone will not enable you to master these complex feelings, and you certainly can't think your way through them. But with some awareness and insight about how those feelings operate, you will deepen your insights about how you define conflict and can start engaging it with more understanding and skill.

Returning to the Five Conflict Scenarios

As you read the previous sections of the chapter, we hope that you gained some insight about the definitions you bring to conflict and some humility about the emotional complexities that conflicts spark for you. Now it's time to put the two pieces together, by thinking and feeling your way through the five conflict scenarios.

Grab your notes to develop these foundational skills further. In doing so, you'll also be able to start your work on the critical tool of perspective-taking, developing an understanding of how one's perspective impacts the conflicts we create and engage.

Scenario One

A parent from another classroom rolls down their car window and begins berating you for a political bumper sticker on your car.

Here are some typical first reactions that participants have shared when we've presented this scenario at conference sessions:

"They need to mind their own business."

"That's their problem, not mine."

"I'm entitled to have and express my political opinion."

"This is my car; I get to choose what to put on it."

"I'm just trying to go to work, not get into an argument!"

"It's not a problem because I don't know that person."

"They have no right to confront me."

"Well, I suppose it is a conflict, but I would just choose to ignore them."

That's when we start asking about definitions: what exactly is the conflict here? While many people agree that the parent is unnecessarily initiating a conflict, people often also point out that a political bumper sticker is provocation—it calls out for others to either agree or disagree with the given political perspective. And that presents a question that begs to be answered: how responsible are we for reactions we evoke when we did not intend to do so? We'll return to this question about intent versus impact throughout the book.

Back to the scenario. Consider your comfort level in engaging in this conflict. What did it feel like when you first read it? We've received mixed responses here too. Some people say they'd dive into this conflict: since you don't work directly with this parent, they say, the risk of relationship consequences is low. Yet other people would not engage in the conflict for the very same reason: the person is a stranger, so you have no responsibility to engage. And doing so would feel risky; you don't know whether or how the situation could escalate.

How do your responses compare to these two ends of the engagement spectrum? Did you have any similar reactions?

We include this scenario to start the discussion of defining conflict. We also include it because it helps to illustrate the importance of intent versus impact. We assume that few readers of this book actively seek to evoke anger, fear, and frustration. Unfortunately, intent and impact rarely match, and that lack of alignment doesn't relieve us of our responsibility to recognize the impact our actions have on others.

The scenario also raises very real feelings of safety (I'm in my car and can drive away) or danger (what if someone is in front of me and I can't get away from an irate person?). When these different responses arise, we start peeling away at the assumptions behind them with some provocative questions. What is this person's gender? Race? Size? What are they driving? What do you assume your bumper sticker says? What do you assume the driver of the other car is saying?

Questions that explore the details we fill into these largely empty scenarios help us get below the surface of our iceberg and tap the meanings, values, and relationships we insert. Similarly, questions about what this scenario evokes emotionally get at a range of feelings from boredom to annoyance to fear to rage. And it's no surprise that people's unique life experiences, reaching back to their childhoods, help establish whether this encounter unfolds within our sense of safety or pushes us out of it.

As with all conflicts, our engagement in and response to conflict is entangled with the "you" we bring to the conflict—and with the "you" that the other person brings. Perhaps they value buying from American companies and you drive a Toyota; perhaps they are stressed about a situation at home or work. There's no way to know.

Scenario Two

Your co-teacher has removed child-centered art without asking you.

Boy, does this scenario get early childhood educators energized! Here are some common, and deeply felt, responses:

"Sure it's a conflict! They had no reason for taking down my artwork."

"Come on. It's no big deal; it's just artwork."

"It's rude. They should've asked first."

"Honestly, I'd just ask them why they took it down."

Defining the conflict for most folks was very straightforward: the other teacher didn't ask you before taking the artwork down. But asking about whether folks would be comfortable engaging in the conflict always produces a flurry of responses—and, to be honest, we don't believe all of them.

For example, many participants have said something like, "Sure, I'd be comfortable bringing this up. I mean, it wouldn't really be a conflict; it would just be a simple conversation!" In our experiences as center directors, we've heard early childhood educators say things like that many times, and yet somehow most of these simple non-conflicts never get addressed at all. Instead, it seems that the situations are actually very complicated and uncomfortable, so much so that teachers try to overlook them or "let them go."

We are convinced that this situation occurs countless times in early childhood programs every day, and that, when it does, those occurrences have the cumulative effect of throwing kindling on fire. Indeed, in our pre-session surveys of participants, when we ask what provokes most workplace conflicts, the overwhelming choice is "the small stuff escalates." Misunderstandings become relationship-killers; repeated errors become insults; failures to recognize one thing or another become disrespect.

So what's under the surface here? Is the removal of the art an honest mistake, or does it reveal complex power dynamics in the classroom? Do team members have different understandings of program philosophy or child development? Who has the authority to make what changes? Do age, longevity, position, or credentialing matter? Is one teacher a favorite of the director or family?

And how explicitly are those power dynamics addressed? Are there defined expectations for different positions? Do people follow them? Are teams really working collaboratively, or do folks just stay in their lanes? Do people avoid talking about those dynamics and instead act them out by moving stuff around?

Scenario Three

A recently adopted toddler bursts into an inconsolable tantrum for seemingly no reason.

This scenario almost always has a unanimous, empathetic response grounded in our knowledge as early childhood educators about child development and the impact of trauma.

"He's going through a lot right now, it makes sense that he's crying."

"Our job is to help children with all of their emotions even if they are expressed abruptly."

"Children cry; it's part of how they communicate."

We know that the child is making very big transitions and that emotional outbursts are common. We are keenly aware of our responsibility to children, which includes helping them process these sorts of big emotions.

That said, we know that many teachers find it difficult to be with children in distress. Despite knowing about the importance of attachment, teachers can find it hard to form those critical bonds that support young children when situations evoke deep-seated emotional risks. If anger and sadness are not emotions you are comfortable with, how might you react to a raging tantrum? If you're feeling sad about challenging life events, how might you react to a sobbing child?

And what happens if the distressed person is an adult? We have found that, overall, folks are significantly more understanding of and patient with children immersed in overwhelming emotions than with adults in the same situation. When children are distressed, we often try to connect by saying, "What's wrong?" But when adults are distressed, we sometimes keep our distance and expect them to get it together.

Finally, think about this scenario and answer the central questions of the chapter: *Is this a conflict? For whom? In what way? How can you be "in" this conflict?*

Scenario Four

An employee bursts into your office and angrily confronts you, charging discrimination.

This scenario produces a mix of responses:

"Depends on if I actually did discriminate against that person."

"Absolutely. Discrimination has to be addressed."

"It's probably a misunderstanding."

In our sessions, we like to say that it can be tricky to determine whether something is a conflict, but this is an easy one: this scenario is absolutely, utterly a conflict. This is the only time we tell people there is a "right" answer to the question, "Is this a conflict?" This scenario highlights a key insight about intent versus impact: whatever one's intent, a declaration that your impact has been discriminatory means you're in a conflict whether you like it or not.

Now and then, a handful of people will lean into intent and try the "not my circus" defense: they didn't mean to do anything discriminatory; it was unintentional or a misunderstanding; the person claiming discrimination is being too sensitive. Those positions are wrong and dangerous. Claims of workplace discrimination require enacting your organization's procedures for such claims, usually based on state and federal law, and doing so immediately is the best and only course of action.

So while we hope our strategies have great value in all of the other scenarios, we caution that, when dealing with claims of discrimination, the terms completely change. Reach out to your supervisor or HR department. Document. Find legal and/or personal support. And, please, recognize that—whatever your intent was—you're in a critical conflict.

Scenario Five

You are an instructional coach. A first-grade student repeatedly ignores classroom instructions; you watch the teacher perform the activity for the child.

When we present this scenario, most people agree that it's a conflict. But more than with any other scenario, folks have a hard time determining what exactly the conflict is.

"Yes, but the child should be following directions."

"Maybe. Does the teacher understand the facilitation expectations?"

"The coach needs to tell the teacher what to do."

Is the coach doing something wrong or inappropriate? Is the teacher? Should the coach correct the teacher? Is the teacher trying to do it "right"? Who gets to decide? Whose perspective should we prioritize: the coach's or the teacher's?

After allowing folks to debate that last question for a while, we often have to point out that, in fact, there's a third perspective to take into account: the child's. What might be happening for this child? What sorts of power dynamics are in play here for this child's experience regarding compliance, teacher-led activities, and developmentally appropriate practice? What does it feel like to have someone else step in to complete an activity for you?

> Early childhood professionals who are immersed in conflict unfailingly erase the children on whom the conflict is supposedly based.

Often, participants respond to these questions with stunned silence. Our adult conflicts can easily overshadow a child's experience, so much so that being reminded of that experience is shocking. How often have classroom colleagues decided to give each other the silent treatment without considering the impact on the children in the room? When have lasting petty differences between teachers poisoned the classroom environment for the children they serve?

While debates about child compliance, developmentally appropriate practice, and coaching methods are certainly part of this scenario, we want to end the chapter by raising up what, for us, is a central issue that prompted this book. Early childhood professionals who are immersed in conflict unfailingly erase the children on whom the conflict is supposedly based.

That means that, whenever we are defining conflict, we need to take care to expand our perspective to include not only the other adults but also the children involved. Yes, if someone declares a situation to be a conflict, then it is indeed a conflict. But children's voices are often quiet or silent, and that means that an adult advocate has to declare and define a conflict on their behalf. It's our responsibility as early childhood educators to engage children's understanding and emotions about the conflict to the best of our ability.

It's hard to reflect on all these pieces: your own perspective, your counterpart's, and—critically—those of the children and families we serve. As you've reflected, we hope you've made your peace with a few takeaways. It's a conflict if someone says it's a conflict. There's no one size fits all; we're constantly resizing. As a result, every conflict is an opportunity to learn. And, yes, this stuff isn't easy.

These reflections help us see how our experiences can shape our reactivity, and that can help us learn how to respond with intelligence and care. In chapter 2, we look at how to prepare useful responses as we dig deeper into conflict.

FROM REACTION TO RESPONSE

Last chapter, our goal was to highlight the importance of defining conflict with precision, not only your own definition but that of others. As we did so, we nudged you further into self-reflection, exploring who the "you" is that you bring into conflict. Now we're going to dive more deeply into reflection, not only to look inward at our own reactivity but also to develop more skillful responses for the conflicts we face.

Making a shift from reaction to response is the precursor to everything else in the book. As we detailed in chapter 1, you bring all of your complicated meanings, values, and relationships into your conflicts, and you usually do so while experiencing core emotions like fear, anger, and shame. When you feel those threats, you activate parts of your brain that are central to survival. And while they are excellent for reacting quickly to threats like approaching lions, tigers, and bears, those parts of your brain aren't built for self-reflection, logic, and composure. Learning to recognize your reactivity, to pause for a breath or two, and to consider a response is therefore essential to finding your way through conflict.

Again, we ask you to do a brief assignment to help you down this path. Write down a narrative describing a recent conflict. You won't be sharing this with anyone but yourself, so pick a rich, powerful, tricky one, as that will be the most productive for this exercise.

It can be personal or work-related; it can be with a child or an adult. It's important that you actually write this down and include as much detail as you can. The details are key because you'll return to what you've written, not to what you remember or think about the conflict. How you tell your story matters!

Take five minutes to write that descriptive narrative. Paint as vivid a picture as you can. Now set it aside.

In this chapter, we encourage you to explore what you've just written as a sort of autobiography, one written in a language that may be hard to understand at first but that we will help you translate. Our translation tool is a set of four questions that will help you learn who you are in conflict and, with that understanding, start to gather your tool kit for conflict engagement and resolution. These questions will be valuable not only for this conflict but also for developing your skills in future conflicts.

What's more, the activities in this chapter are excellent for developing conflict skills in teams. The narratives folks write are, by definition, very personal, but the activities all maintain confidentiality—you never share the details. Instead, those details provide a way to talk about more general issues that are part of every conflict.

We've found that this sort of shared self-reflection is invaluable for everyone working in an early childhood setting, but especially for coaches, administrators, and others in leadership positions that demand a lot of interaction in tricky situations. So if you're thinking about ways to put these activities into action at your workplace, consider doing them with others. It's actually pretty fun!

It's also a bit risky, we admit. So we'll take that risk with you.

Chris and Christine Share Their Conflicts

To help you unpack your own narrative, we feel it's only fair to unpack ours with you. While yours will always stay private, we are voluntarily revealing ours, with permission from the identifiable person involved in Christine's conflict (a colleague) and identifying information removed from Chris's conflict.

And we're not going to take the easy way out. Both of us regularly find ourselves to be awkward or hesitant in certain conflicts, and we've found those imperfect efforts to be the most useful ones to explore. We also provide a lot of support to each other in our explorations, recognizing the shared humanness revealed in our botched efforts or flawed understandings.

Most importantly, by developing a greater understanding of who we are in conflict, we have learned how to become the responsive people we want to be in conflict, and not the people our history and reactivity bring to conflict. It's not easy, but it works.

First, here's Christine's conflict.

I was a toddler teacher in a large program during a time of turnover in leadership. I had worked in the program for several years and had strong relationships with my peers, though I was not in a leadership role. My colleagues trusted me to coordinate and communicate on their behalf, and I was happy to do it.

On one occasion, the program director from the other side of the building had to step in and create a break schedule for us because we were short-staffed. She walked into my classroom and handed me the schedule for the day—but it was all wrong. I took one look at it, dropped it on the desk, said "Whatever," and went back to teaching.

I was annoyed that I had to take a different break than usual, and even more annoyed that she didn't talk to me before creating the schedule. I could've helped her if she had bothered to seek my input! I huffed and puffed about this for the rest of the day. And I struggled to make eye contact with her the next time I saw her. I felt disrespected and disregarded.

Here's Chris's conflict.

For weeks, our school team had been working with a parent to sort out how best to support their toddler's transition to a preschool classroom. The teachers had shared information with them at arrival and departure; the family advocate had met with them repeatedly to determine how things were going at home.

But then the child started engaging in behavior that created hygiene problems for other children and the teachers. As things seemed to be escalating, I decided that it was time to meet with the parent to find ways to address both the new behavior and our preschool readiness concerns.

As always, I wanted to make sure that we were very organized. So I created a point-by-point agenda for our meeting, with explicit goals for moving forward. I made sure to invite everyone on our team who could be a resource, although the teacher couldn't be there due to a scheduling conflict. Finally, I debriefed everyone one-on-one so we were all on the same page.

It was hard work to prepare for the meeting, but I felt proud of myself and my team. We were putting everything on the table to demonstrate transparency and build trust, and were all truly prepared to do whatever we could. Walking into work on the big day, I knew that I had done everything possible to have a successful meeting focused on supporting this family.

But it was a disaster!

Despite all of my plans, I lost control of the meeting almost immediately. The parent brought an advocate to the meeting who grilled us about the agenda, throwing us all off guard. I had created it so that we could find solutions together, but they were convinced that I had other intentions.

Over and over, I kept trying to clarify that we were there to support the child, as my team nodded anxiously in support. Then suddenly the parent blurted out, "We know that you're just going to kick him out."

It was like a punch in the stomach for all of us! My team fumbled around awkwardly for several minutes, and the meeting ended with things much, much worse than they were just a few days before. After the parent and advocate left, we all looked at each other with blank stares.

I was shocked: I had worked so hard with our team to build the perfect meeting to support the family, yet all the parent could see was a conspiracy to expel the child! Meanwhile, my team was distraught. How in the world had this happened?

Reflection Questions

Now, with your and our conflict narratives ready, we can start to develop our responsive tool kit. The rest of the chapter is structured around four key questions that we've asked hundreds of workshop participants to consider as they analyze their conflict narratives. These questions have two purposes. First, they'll help you understand the shape of your own individual reactivity. By asking these questions about the narratives, you'll get a chance to see where your brain goes in conflict. Second, these questions make excellent prompts to insert into your future reactivity during conflict, allowing you to pause, reflect, and recognize better ways to respond.

1. **Whose perspective** did your words reflect the most: yours or the other person's?

2. In your transcription of the conflict, did you spend more time on the **emotional** experience of the conflict or how it ended, the **outcome**?

3. Did you spend more time on **intent** or **impact**?

4. Think back to the conflict itself, what was your comfort level with the tension? Were you fully **immersed in** the moment of conflict or **hurrying to get out** of it?

Let's tackle each question with our conflict narratives close at hand. For extra support, we provide some thoughts about how workshop participants have responded to these questions.

Whose Perspective?

As you can tell from our personal narratives, we—and the vast majority of workshop participants over the years—focused our attention on our own perspectives.

That means, of course, that we were not focusing on the perspectives of the individuals with whom we were in conflict. Christine didn't bother to consider or ask for an explanation from her colleague. Meanwhile, Chris talked to everyone on the planet about how best to structure that meeting—everyone, that is, except for the parent who was the focus of the meeting.

These are merely two examples of a key determining factor in nearly every conflict we have ever experienced or considered. In conflict, most of us focus on our own perspective, supporting it with more and more evidence that we see things the way that they ought to be seen. It's like a traditional Japanese saying: if we look at the sky through a bamboo pole, all we see is a small circle instead of the vast perspective outside the circle.

This is a particularly important element of the self-awareness needed to develop our conflict engagement and resolution skills to better serve children. Despite this tendency to focus on ourselves, adults often ask children in conflict, "How do you think the other child feels?" This question is likely an effort to *help* them consider the other person's perspective, but to our ears it often sounds like shaming a child for *not* seeing the other person's side of the situation, and, in doing so, overlooking the developmental limitations for children to shift perspective.

There is more later in the book on this essential skill of perspective-taking. But, for now, it is important to develop the preliminary skill of recognizing that we are peering through a bamboo pole and thus failing to see the whole picture.

Emotion or Outcome?

The development of social and emotional skills is a lot like the philosophy of process versus product in art: the learning and value doesn't happen at the end, it happens throughout the entire experience. Often in conflict, we want to jump to the conclusion, or, when working with children, we want to provide the answer for them. This is called a *righting reflex,* a strong desire to make things right when we see a problem. This reflex is common among early childhood educators in our work with children, but fixing things fundamentally robs children of exactly what we are committed to doing: guiding them to learn and develop.

As early childhood education professionals, we are passionate about caring for others, and this drive is meant to be helpful. When a problem pops up, we instinctively draw on our years of experience that help us easily recognize a solution that will work for everyone. But the process versus product distinction above is as true for children as it is for adults. Learning how to get better at engaging and resolving conflicts comes from working through them, not from being provided with an answer.

The consistent pattern that we've noticed in our workshops during this reflection activity is that, even after a conflict is over and people are describing it, people almost never write about the amazing solution that they identified. Instead, they write about their emotions, how mad, sad, offended, or angry they were. No one needs to share how the conflict ended; people need to convince others how it felt to be in it.

Christine's frustration is the focus of her narrative: everyone got a break that day, but that's not even included in her narrative. The outcome didn't matter as much as her emotional reaction and its related values concerning communication, responsibility, and respect. Similarly, Chris's narrative emphasizes his pride in diligence, preparation, and integrity. As for the disastrous outcome, well, he doesn't know how to respond!

> When we focus too much on the outcome for ourselves or children, we miss the emotional learning part that will help us engage in conflict better in the future.

We've learned over the years that the same is true for most people. Even when a conflict is over, our energy goes back to the emotions we experienced rather than the outcome. That is, even when a conflict is resolved, we can still get caught up in rehashing what it felt like to be in it. Thus, it is necessary to commit to the process of engaging in conflict rather than trying to fast-forward to the solution. When we focus too much on the outcome for ourselves or children, we miss the emotional learning part that will help us engage in conflict better in the future.

Intent or Impact?

Distinguishing between intent and impact is a crucial skill for being in conflict. And if you ever needed proof, just take a look at Chris's story.

Throughout his narrative, Chris emphasizes good intentions, hard effort, professional preparation, and individual support. Over and over, he provides evidence that he and his team were doing the right thing, on the parent's side, and exhibiting values like honesty and transparency. "I knew that I had done everything possible," he writes—a statement that, we now know, is simply not true.

Like most of us in conflict, Chris exhibits his defensiveness in his dogged commitment to explaining his intent. *Buts* are implied throughout, as if he's protesting to the judge and jury about his innocence. Just imagine:

- But I made sure that we were very organized!

- But I created a point-by-point agenda for our meeting!

- But I made sure to invite everyone on our team who could be a resource!

- But I debriefed everyone one-on-one so that we were all on the same page!

- But we were putting everything on the table to demonstrate transparency and build trust!

- But we were all truly prepared to do whatever we could!

We've learned over the years that this dogged commitment to intent is nearly always a sign that something is out of whack—a sign that we regularly ignore because, well, we're doing the best we can. So it takes a lot of time and energy to learn how to switch your focus from your intentions to the impact of your actions.

It's quite a paradox. It seems at first that the one thing you can control is your intention and that the impact of your actions is out of your hands. But that's only true if you focus on the moment of the conflict itself. If you can focus on the outcome, on the impact your actions had on someone else, you can have tremendous control over your response as well as time to formulate it clearly—and thereby help shape the on-going impact of your actions.

Focusing on the outcome has another benefit: it's the light at the end of the tunnel. If you're in a conflict, chances are good that you've screwed up in one way or another; the impact of your actions hasn't been ideal or even positive. So this is the time to remember one of our core principles: conflict is normal, natural, and deeply human. Social psychologists like to refer to interpersonal conflict as rupture, a sudden breach of an otherwise harmonious relationship. They pair rupture with repair, emphasizing that, whatever the problem, most times there are opportunities to regain what trust or intimacy was lost.

We believe that you'll be better able to move from reaction to response if, in the midst of a rupture, you take a moment to remember that repair is possible. We are often so focused on the moment of the conflict itself that we can't see future moments in which the conflict is no longer the dominant feature. Framing conflicts using rupture and repair reminds us that conflicts are a part of life, and they do not define a terminal moment after which all possibilities die.

This is one of the wonderful consolations of learning how to work more effectively with conflict. Nearly every conflict, major and minor, provides a chance to rebuild trust, strengthen connection, and move forward collaboratively. Nearly every rupture gives us a chance for repair.

Of course, if you get stuck in your *buts*, then you'll never see past your reaction to the rupture and get to a responsive repair. And, as you'll see in the next chapter, those *buts* can be very sticky indeed.

Being In or Getting Out?

We always end this exercise in our workshops with this question: Thinking back to the conflict itself, what was your comfort level with the tension? Were you fully immersed in the moment of conflict or hurrying to get out of it?

Here's why this matters. Conflict is going to keep popping up. It is going to be emotional and difficult. You are going to keep being *you* in conflict. And you can be your most authentic self when you trust yourself to be able to sit in it for as long as it takes.

Given that you picked up this book, chances are you fall into one of two different personality tendencies: perhaps you are conflict-engaging, eager to build your skills, or perhaps you are conflict-averse, trying to figure how you can manage situations you desperately want to avoid. Regardless of your entry point into this work, your commitment to engagement will result in growth in your skillset and subsequent growth in your relationships.

For Chris, the conflict with the parent meeting revealed an unpleasant insight. While he likes to think of himself as conflict-engaging—to the point of co-writing this book about it— the parent meeting conflict demonstrates that he is sometimes more interested in convincing himself that he's done a great job of engaging conflict when he's actually avoiding it. After all, the parent was the main person Chris needed to engage, not his staff. The time and energy he devoted to staging the meeting was, in fact, more of a performance of conflict engagement than the real deal.

Christine, like Chris, wants to believe that she is conflict-engaging and that, through years of practice, she is comfortable being in conflict. However, Christine was avoiding her role in the conflict by acting like there wouldn't be one if her colleague had simply met her expectations. The reality is, Christine's reactiveness amplified the conflict rather than facilitating resolution—and was the exact opposite of what we guide people in conflict to do.

From Reaction to Response

So given these reactive challenges, how should we respond when conflicts arise?

By now we hope you know that, as you find a path through conflict, there's no premade roadmap available. No formula is flawless in every situation; no technique is the magic solution. Instead, what works is having a set of questions, perspectives, and skills on hand, tools you will bring to bear as the situation demands.

In one sense, conflicts are like young children. We have to be very careful when we assess them, paying attention to the biases we bring and the perspectives we emphasize. No assessment tool captures the whole child, so we need to use all of our analytical skills in combination—and with a healthy dose of humility. Finally, child assessment is never about this moment; it's about all of the moments moving forward, the developmental trajectory each individual child is on.

The same is true for conflict: we need to know our stuff, observe the conflict carefully, and make responsive decisions that support development and growth. And as our narratives reveal all too well, part of our response involves reflecting on our reaction. We can't *stay* in our reaction; it's the worst possible position from which to respond. But we need to sit in our reactivity to be able to respond with insight, care, and responsibility. And, given the value of humility in nearly every conflict, it's a good way to remind yourself that you're just an imperfect person doing the best you can.

Here are a few tips to keep in mind as you move from reaction to response.

Ask "Whose Perspective?" and Add the Missing Ones

As shown repeatedly above, you are likely to get stuck in your perspective when you're in a conflict. No need to beat yourself up about it—you're human, after all. But don't stay stuck.

Instead, when you recognize that's happening, it's best to ask yourself explicitly, "Whose perspective am I missing?" Chances are that your counterpart is the key omission—but keep an eye out for people at the margins who may not be speaking up very loudly. In our profession, those folks are often parents or children, and given our commitment to serve them, it's only right to consider their perspective when things are going wrong.

Admit Intent, But Focus on Impact

You need to own your story, and that means admitting that your intent is part of the conflict. But focusing on intent gets in the way of perceiving impact, as we've seen, and your defensiveness will keep turning your attention to your intentions, reasoning, justifications, and the like.

So you need to tap your better self on the shoulder and ask, "What is the impact of all of these well-intentioned actions?" Often, that just means learning how to hear without your defensive earplugs in. Most of the time, your counterpart is being pretty clear about that impact, if only you take a deep breath and listen.

Spend Time Learning Within the Conflict—Don't Hurry Out

For many years, our workshop title was "Being IN to Get OUT of Conflict," simply because we knew that folks were rushing to leave the unpleasantness as quickly as possible. That advice is still sound.

Conflicts are opportunities to learn about yourself, about another person, and about our shared humanity. If you can spend time in conflicts, you'll develop a deeper understanding of who you are—and, we sincerely hope, some tolerance, humility, and self-deprecating humor about the foibles we all share.

Go Ahead, Apologize—But Don't Spend Too Much Time on It

Until recently, we often blurted out "Don't apologize" in our workshops. Apologizing is usually a way to avoid, not engage, the person we've hurt or saddened or frustrated. Now we feel a bit more tolerant of these moments of confession. But make it snappy: most of the time, your counterpart is looking for action, not words. There is nothing more frustrating in a conflict than watching another person beat themselves up, as if doing so solves anything. Repair requires collaboration, and spending time on apologies and self-flagellation just puts off that work for later—a later that, sometimes, never arrives.

And given that children need us to model the work of engaging in conflict, *sorry* can be very complicated for them to interpret. Adults often seek expressions of remorse from others, requiring children to say "sorry," for example. Those performances of manners avoid our responsibility to teach children how to engage conflict resolution, which includes perspective-taking and articulating the details of the conflict to reach a solution. It can also confuse children into using a quick-fix script to gloss over tension rather than developing true empathy for others.

Acknowledge Rupture and Commit to Repairing Broken Trust

The power of simply stating, "We are in a conflict" out loud is profound. Suddenly, there is a thing that is separate from you, your identity, your integrity. It doesn't activate blame; the "we" points no fingers. Instead, "we are in a conflict" announces that the situation is just a problem, and a very human one. And given that everyone involved is a human, it's an opportunity for connection.

So acknowledge the rupture. Admit reality out loud. This spares all parties the ambiguity of what is happening in the relationship. And then, after a deep breath, state a commitment to repairing the trust that has been broken. Simply doing so will begin that process of repair.

Express and Exhibit Patience

Remember the righting reflex! We in the helping professions are prone to relying upon quick fixes, handing out fish left and right instead of teaching people how to fish. But just as we should with children, we need to recognize that adult development requires patience.

Broken relationships don't get fixed overnight, and declarations that "everything is fine" get in the way of the work required for repair. So declare that repair will take time, and commit to the patient engagement that repair requires.

Chris and Christine Respond to Their Conflicts

Since it's hard to apply these tips in a generic, abstract sense, we want to present our responses in detail as concrete examples of how we responded to the two situations described above.

Chris's Response

Chris and his team used the reflection questions introduced at the beginning of this chapter to consider what had happened in the catastrophic meeting with the parent. The team realized that they had a lot of repair work to do, and Chris knew that, as school director, it had to start at the top. So, two days after the meeting, he sent out the following email to the parent (identifying information has been removed).

Dear Parent,

As our team reflected on our meeting last week, we arrived at the conclusion that we inadvertently created a situation that made that meeting hard and put you in an unfair and difficult situation. So I'm writing to apologize.

I made several critical mistakes in the lead-up to the meeting. In gathering the information from our team, I should have made a distinction between the broad developmental concerns about which we wanted to collaborate with you and the hygiene issues that had arisen. That was wrong.

Having the family advocate reach out to you about a "hard conversation" with a detailed agenda communicated exactly the opposite of what we had hoped it would, suggesting a heartless severity instead of an empathetic sharing of frames and resources. Failing to have the teacher at the meeting meant that your important questions could not be answered in the very situation we had created.

Finally, my facilitation of the meeting did not make you feel heard, understood, or respected.

It's no wonder that our attempt to build transparency and trust did exactly the opposite. I am truly sorry that it happened, and I want us to do all that we can moving forward to rebuild trust. So, if you are willing to do so, I'd like to propose that we try again in the not-too-distant future to have the conversation we failed to have last week.

Please expect members of our team to begin reaching out to you to think together about what our next steps can and should be. I ask that you be blunt and directive when that happens; we feel like our team has made a mess of communication thus far and want this reset to respond to your and your family's needs.

After a few weeks of repairing what we've broken, I hope that we can find a way to sit down together and turn our attention to your child's needs in the coming months and years.

Sincerely,
Chris

As I [Chris] think back on this situation, I can't help but realize how powerful it was to think through the four questions above and address them directly. The result was an email that focused entirely on the parent's perspective, one that made no attempt whatsoever to defend my actions. Many of the sentences quote their criticisms directly, reframing them as truths that I needed to admit and accept.

Put differently, I knew that I had been blinded by my intentions, and that my inability to perceive the impact of my actions created much of the problem. Thus, the email set aside intent entirely, focusing solely on the impact that our communication, the agenda, and the meeting had on the family.

Finally, and most importantly, the email was about being immersed in the conflict and not yet another plan for getting out of it. I didn't attach an agenda that I had written; I didn't impose next steps that I had conceived. Rather, I indicated how we would repair what was broken, a process that required time, collaboration, and patience.

That all sounds so reasonable, doesn't it? But I must admit that I hated—*hated*—writing that email! I hated that I had botched the situation so thoroughly. I hated that I was blind to all of my reactivity masking as good, hard work. I hated the whole, appalling mess. And yet I knew I had to confront all of my misunderstandings, blind spots, and hubris if I truly wanted to repair the relationship.

Of course, the email wasn't a magic wand that transformed the mess into a glorious, trusting situation. However, by confronting these questions, I not only began to rebuild that broken relationship between a family and my school, I also learned more about myself in conflict than I had in years.

It wasn't fun. At all. But I'm grateful for the remarkably valuable insights, to which I've returned again and again.

Christine's Response

I [Christine] wish I had a well-constructed being-in-conflict letter to share with you regarding my response to the scheduling conflict with my colleague, but I don't. I did consider the prompts, and I do have some powerful reflections and a follow-up conversation to share with you.

When I read back through this narrative, I have three significant thoughts, in this order: Wow, I didn't realize I was so passive-aggressive. It stings a little to consider how hurtful I was to someone I barely knew, over something very solvable. I'm a little embarrassed to admit in writing that my desire to be seen as a knowledgeable, capable colleague overpowered my ability to be in productive discussion.

Second, I didn't include my colleague's perspective *at all*. I wasn't productively engaging in conflict; I tried to tuck it away with indignance and shame—which as we all know was just going to resurface, either in this same conflict or fueling another conflict.

Finally, that interaction was a make-or-break moment in my career. Months later, I was up for a promotion at a different site, and this woman was being considered for promotion to a leadership role at that site and would potentially be my supervisor—but only if we could work through our differences. We did, and when I paused and considered her perspective I learned that she deeply cares about input from others and she was quite overwhelmed at the moment of our initial interaction over scheduling. She learned that I am indeed good at scheduling, and that became my task in our new roles. We went on to work together closely in many capacities over the next fifteen years. But that required reflection, vulnerability, and taking the time to work through conflict together.

Your Turn

That's how the two of us took the next steps in the conflicts we had created or exacerbated. Sharing those—first with each other, and now with you—felt risky; exposing all of those foibles and screw-ups makes us both feel vulnerable. But taking the risk of vulnerability gave us access to new understanding, not only individually but in dialogue. We think it's worth it.

So let's turn back to your conflict. Reread what you wrote and carefully consider the reflection questions:

1. **Whose perspective** did your words reflect the most: yours or the other person's?

2. In your transcription of the conflict, did you spend more time on the **emotional** experience of the conflict or how it ended, the **outcome**?

3. Did you spend more time on **intent** or **impact**?

4. Think back to the conflict itself, what was your comfort level with the tension? Were you fully **immersed in** the moment of conflict or **hurrying to get out** of it?

Now, like we did, reflect on what you learned.

- Which of the responses to conflict are ones you want to work on?

- Identify perspectives beyond your own.

- Admit intent, but focus on impact.

- Spend time learning within the conflict. Don't hurry out.

- Apologize—but don't spend too much time on it.

- Acknowledge rupture and commit to repairing broken trust.

- Express and exhibit patience.

If this feels hard, you're not alone. Some researchers refer to this work as the inherent stickiness of all conflict. So that's where we turn next. Prepare to get unstuck.

CHAPTER 3

CONFLICT IS STICKY

Conflict is sticky. *Stickiness* is a concept used in fields like communication, psychology, and marketing to describe the ways in which certain messages or meanings "stick" to us. A hashtag that resonates within a community and becomes a bond that draws them together; a way of explaining a complex concept simply and effectively, such that people use it to understand themselves and the world; that meme, movie scene, or pop song hook that you just can't shake from your brain: all of those things are sticky, whether we want them to be or not.

> *Stickiness* is a concept used in fields like communication, psychology, and marketing to describe the ways in which certain messages or meanings "stick" to us.

Conflict is sticky in that same way. Over and over, when a conflict arises at work, we promise ourselves that we'll leave it there at the end of the day, that we won't bring it home to our families and loved ones. But often that just doesn't work, and we find ourselves spending a bit too much time at dinner talking angrily about a frustrating encounter in a hallway or waking up at 2:00 a.m. replaying an email exchange that happened twelve hours earlier. While we may tell ourselves we are going to let it go and move on, sometimes our brains have other ideas.

So, to find our way through conflict, we need to learn more about—and from—these sticky elements that clump together.

Learning from Stickiness

In this chapter, we ask you to honor stickiness, to approach it as—you guessed it—an opportunity to learn. That you've gotten this far in the book is a demonstration of your commitment to turning toward difficult, challenging situations. So, once again, we ask you to do the same, this time focusing your attention on the elements of conflict that are getting in your way. There is a lot to learn about conflict as you untangle it.

Consider this thought experiment. Look back on your work as an early childhood educator. Identify a child whose social, emotional, and behavioral development has been most difficult to support. This is the child for whom your strategies just didn't work, the child who made you question your self-efficacy as an early childhood educator. No matter how quickly you ran to your car at the end of the day, that child was always sitting in it when you arrived, an invisible, irksome reminder of all that went wrong.

For you, this child is sticky. There are individual details that you can isolate: a spectacularly bad transition, a troubling child outcome assessment, an exhausting afternoon dragging into evening due to a parent's delay. But whatever they might look like written down on a page, those individual details somehow add up to more than the sum of their parts in your brain. For some reason, this particular child is the one who invokes something you just can't shake off.

Here's Christine's sticky kid.

The sticky child in my career didn't start off as sticky. His behavior was initially sweet and playful, and everyone working with him quickly built strong connections with him. He came to us with a complicated backstory, fraught with drastic change and complicated relationships. And yet here he was, in a stable home and school environment, thriving.

As a result, we were all caught off guard when, several months into our care, his behavior started to change. He had emotional outbursts that were hard to predict and support. During those outbursts, his behaviors escalated, becoming a threat to both his own safety and the safety of others.

Our team was well trained in dealing with challenging behaviors, and we went to work, trying all of our strategies to no avail. Meanwhile, we watched as our other relationships faltered. As his challenges increased, so did those of his family; as his behavior escalated, other children in the class were drawn into the challenges, thereby drawing their families in as well. Everyone struggled.

I'd like to end this story by sharing the magic solution that resolved everything, but that's not how it ended. After weeks of frustration in which we repeatedly reviewed the long list of all we had tried but failed to do, we learned that his family was moving out of the area and that he was transitioning to another program. We lost the chance to figure him out; we never learned how to help him.

This child and his unresolved, challenging situation have stuck with me over decades. When I'm wondering whether this is the right career for me, the situation challenges my sense that I am truly a good educator, forgetting the thousands of children I've supported in their growth and learning.

In fact, I carry this one boy into every tricky situation I have with children like him. He's not a reminder of failure, exactly, but rather he serves as a reminder of the perseverance our team dedicated to him and his family, a reminder that we didn't give up. Finally, he also reminds me that some situations are simply unsolvable, not because we aren't capable but because they are genuinely very complex.

Thanks to him, I've learned the value of the sticky kid. He can be frustrating, to be sure, but he is immensely valuable and powerful in my continued career.

We believe that these unforgettable children are incredibly important figures in our lives as educators. They can teach us critical lessons about the values, culture, priorities, and sense of self-worth that we bring into our professional lives. But those lessons are only revealing if we're willing to reflect on the situation to learn about ourselves.

Mindfulness When You're Stuck

To learn about your relationship to conflict, be prepared to shift your attitude. There's simply no way to unpack what are, for you, the sloppiest, lousiest parts of conflict while closing your eyes, holding your nose, and hoping it all goes away. And this confrontation with the worst characteristics of conflict requires, of course, a confrontation with yourself.

To do this, we encourage you to develop a practice of mindfulness. Jon Kabat-Zinn, the founder of the Mindfulness-Based Stress Reduction Clinic at the University of Massachusetts Medical School, defines mindfulness as "paying attention in a particular way: on purpose, in the present moment, and nonjudgmentally" (Kabat-Zinn 1994).

For early childhood educators, responding to a series of challenging, unnerving situations with children, families, and colleagues each day requires paying close, purposeful attention in the moment and without judgment. It is essential to the work. Child assessment demands careful observation in the moment, resisting the leap to judgmental conclusions. Parents interrupt us at arrival to get support for decisions with which we do not necessarily agree. Colleagues do unexpected things that require more time and attention than we often have. Mindfulness helps us do all of that work effectively, intelligently, and compassionately.

Mindfulness practices are widely available to educators these days, and they take many forms.

> For early childhood educators, responding to a series of challenging, unnerving situations with children, families, and colleagues each day requires paying close, purposeful attention in the moment and without judgment.

Both of us maintain our own versions of those practices in our daily lives, and we find them immensely valuable. We encourage you to download the companion PLC from freespirit.com /PLC for more about our approach to mindfulness and how our practices inform our relationships and our paths through conflict.

> Reflection is an essential practice if you want to find your way through conflict. You need to be able to reflect on complex situations, your role in them, and the feelings and sensations that arise in your body when you live through and recall them.

It's been our experience that mindfulness in conflict doesn't just happen if you pay attention in a particular way. For example, humans tend to feel pretty crabby in conflict, and that means that the things our brains select when we "pay attention" end up contributing to conflict instead of helping us find a way through it.

Rather, we have learned that mindfulness in conflict requires us to make an attitude adjustment, shifting our mood, intention, and energy from a negative to a positive engagement with conflict. The following are the four essential attitudes embedded in these mindfulness practices. There is also a quick overview reproducible of them on page 45. You might want to post them somewhere as a reminder when conflicts arise.

The Attitude of Nonjudgmental Reflection

Reflection is an essential practice if you want to find your way through conflict. You need to be able to reflect on complex situations, your role in them, and the feelings and sensations that arise in your body when you live through and recall them. Many of the exercises we've done so far have asked you to reflect purposefully. In particular, the reflective activity in chapter 1 asks you to consider how you experience challenging emotions in your current conflicts. In addition, other questions ask you to reflect on specific components of conflict and the traits you bring to bear in them.

The attitude of nonjudgmental reflection is listed first to highlight the importance of developing the ability—the attitude—to reflect without judgment on the people involved in your conflict. Let's take your counterpart. It's just a fact: to sort out the conflict you've co-created, you'll need to be able to see your counterpart as another flawed human being, one with whom you have a lot more in common than not. (Apologies if this fact comes as a disappointment.)

This fact is relevant in most every conflict. Sure, other people have contributed to the conflict—but so have you; sure, they could respond to the situation better—but so could you. We are all flawed. The challenge is to find a way to reflect on the situation and others in it without jumping to the judgments your brain is hardwired to encourage. (More on that hardwiring later in the chapter.)

Like all of these attitudes, nonjudgmental reflection sounds simple enough on paper, but it is difficult stuff. And we've learned over the years that many early childhood educators are able to approach situations and other people with a seemingly generous "let it go" approach. Instead of stepping into the conflict, they decide it's not that big a deal, that the other person means well, and that it's best to move on.

While that sounds pleasant enough, we fear that those little conflicts often escalate due to being avoided. We also suspect that there's something more complicated happening under the surface: the person who is so happy to "let it go" is actually reluctant to confront what the conflict has to say about a lot of things—including about them.

That is to say: the nonjudgmental reflection that is most challenging for those folks isn't refraining from criticizing others. It's refraining from criticizing and judging themselves. Time and again, we have encountered educators who are quick to point out their own faults, always ready to apologize for and explain all that they've done wrong in any given situation. It's as if there's a mean-spirited critic sitting on their shoulder all day long, whispering relentless criticism, and any conflict they encounter confirms those lousy judgments.

That's why we think the attitude of *nonjudgmental* reflection is essential. After all, when you look at what makes conflict sticky for you, it's not going to be pretty. But if that reflection simply piles another layer of self-judgment onto the situation, you're not finding your way through conflict—you're just handing more popcorn to that movie critic on your shoulder.

Thankfully, there's a second attitude that will help you handle any debilitating self-judgment that gets in your way.

The Attitude of Humble Curiosity

Since you've made it this far in the book, we're going to assume that, like us, conflict makes you curious. As authors of a book on the subject, we're certainly prejudiced on this point, but we think conflict is endlessly fascinating.

As we delve into conflict, we've learned the hard way that it's best to embrace an attitude of humility. Over and over, as our curiosity leads us down some new path, we have our deeply held assumptions overturned and our strong initial conclusions questioned. Thankfully, the two of us have a trustworthy relationship in which we can reliably call each other out if that curiosity isn't tempered by humility.

In fact, we have become especially curious about situations—like our examples in chapter 2—in which we are anything but humble. When we become arrogant, convinced of the accuracy of our positions, we lean into each other and try to pry loose that arrogance with humility. That's a practice that comes with experience: the more we learn about conflict, the more we learn how little we know.

In the world of social science research, this attitude of humble curiosity has a slightly different name: intellectual humility. Researchers have taken up this subject in light of problems revealed within our current scientific community, challenging colleagues to learn how to admit when they are wrong.

It's an uphill battle, by all accounts. In his article on the subject, Vox science reporter Brian Resnick lists three challenges on the path to intellectual humility:

> In order for us to acquire more intellectual humility, we all, even the smartest among us, need to better appreciate our cognitive blind spots. Our minds are more imperfect and imprecise than we'd often like to admit. Our ignorance can be invisible.

> Even when we overcome that immense challenge and figure out our errors, we need to remember we won't necessarily be punished for saying, "I was wrong." And we need to be braver about saying it. We need a culture that celebrates those words.

> We'll never achieve perfect intellectual humility. So we need to choose our convictions thoughtfully (Resnick 2019).

Resnick's challenges are very useful. You will find your way through conflict more effectively if you can appreciate your cognitive blind spots. (That includes the biggest blind spot of all, the one in which you are convinced you have no blind spots!) You will engage conflict more effectively if you can take a deep breath and courageously admit your errors.

> **You will engage conflict more effectively if you can take a deep breath and courageously admit your errors.**

The same is true for the last item on Resnick's list. He urges us to "choose our convictions thoughtfully," to recognize that they are indeed convictions, and that convictions and intellectual humility don't help each other very much. When you're in a sticky conflict, it's very important to know that you might be wrong about the things you hold most deeply. And it's even more important to know that your conviction that you are always right is of little use to anyone, including you.

Sounds unpleasant, doesn't it? Fear not! Intellectual humility need not be humiliating. Indeed, the third attitude reveals the jovial side of humble curiosity.

The Attitude of Self-Effacing Humor

When we started the process of shifting our work on conflict from collaboratively performed, workshop-based content to collaboratively written, book-based content, we asked colleagues who had attended our sessions what lively bits might drop out if we weren't careful. Most folks talked about replicating the relationship we share, showing the ways that conflict requires attention to interpersonal flux and flow. Others listed specific exercises that they felt were essential for the book to make sense, all of which are included here.

Those answers we expected. The advice we didn't expect was, "Make sure you're still funny."

We've puzzled over that quite a bit. It's sort of a compliment, we suppose. But it took us a while to figure out what the compliment was all about. After all, we weren't doing stand-up comedy; there were no jokes to speak of. What exactly was so funny?

Then we presented the workshop a few times while also working on the book. During those presentations, we realized that, in fact, there were jokes. Lots of them. But we hadn't noticed at first, because the jokes were on us.

We realized that our workshop relies upon an attitude of self-effacing humor. We poke fun at our miscues, our blind spots, our reactivity, and ourselves. But the more we looked at it, the more we saw that that sense of self-deprecating humor wasn't just a fun, or funny, part of our shtick. In fact, it is an essential part of exploring the stickiest conflicts we confront.

Learning from conflict is hard work for all of us. And the conflicts that have the most to teach us, the stickiest ones, tap our most complex feelings and meanings. Let's be honest: doing that work with a sense of humble reflection can be demoralizing, even downright scary.

Adopting an attitude of self-effacing humor helps undo that fear. Finding our way through conflict can mean we lose our grip on being an assured professional. There we are, bumbling around at our worst—it doesn't really seem like it would be fun or funny to look at. But if we cut ourselves some slack and realize that our bumbling is what makes us human, we gain a bit of cheerful yet mindful distance from those things.

When we approach our sticky conflicts with some mindfulness, we can admit that we are who we are in the moment, and that the moment is a result of a series of causes and conditions, decisions and choices. We'll never untangle all of those factors, to be sure, and that means we're likely to find ourselves in many of the same situations later no matter how hard we try.

It's a repetitive scenario, not without its inherent absurd humor. So why not poke a bit of fun at it, expose that humor for what it is, the sign of our relentless humanity?

The Attitude of Accepting Imperfection

The fourth attitude is a lesson the two of us have learned the hard way, so we hope you'll benefit from our mistakes.

Together, we have over two decades of working to understand conflict. We've spent more time thinking about conflict lately than just about anything else. And we've put what we've learned into practice. We've facilitated many, many conversations with our colleagues, employees, and supervisors. We've delivered conflict workshops across the country for thousands of people. We are willing to roll up our sleeves and take on just about any conflict we meet.

> **Reflective, curious, good-natured engagement with imperfection is endlessly rich and valuable.**

We certainly feel like we've made progress over the years. Sometimes it feels slow; sometimes it feels like we're not really moving. Most of the time, though, even if we feel we're spinning around, we like to think we're progressing. Like viewing a screw from above, we hope spinning means that, slowly but surely, we are drilling further down.

When we first started, we thought that eventually we'd reach expertise, that we'd master conflict. Surely, we thought, after all this time, practice would make perfect. Right?

Wrong.

To be sure, we have learned a lot of helpful insights about ourselves and about strategies that can help us in conflict. We've got a decent tool kit, one that we're sharing with you here. And in a lot of situations, we like to think that we're able to help folks out.

But the most important thing we've learned is that practice will never make perfect. Instead, we know that practice gives us more and more opportunities to learn that our goal should be a more thoughtful engagement with the imperfection that is inherent in all conflicts.

Thankfully, we have ourselves and others, a bunch of similarly imperfect humans, getting into conflicts that lead to imperfect solutions. Now and then we gain a sliver of insight or a newly useful tactic, something that allows us to see that imperfection with a bit more clarity. But we're convinced that practice will never make perfect.

So, if none of us are ever going to master the way through conflict, what do we do? Adopt the attitude that practice makes imperfect. Become good at harnessing all the nonjudgmental reflection, humble curiosity, and self-effacing humor you can muster, and engage in each conflict with a commitment to learning from the practice. Most importantly, perhaps, we want you to accept that perfection is an unattainable, useless fantasy. Reflective, curious, good-natured engagement with imperfection is endlessly rich and valuable.

Quick Overview
The Four Essential Attitudes of Mindfulness

Mindfulness in conflict requires us to make an attitude adjustment, shifting our mood, intention, and energy from a negative to a positive engagement with conflict. The full description of these attitudes is on pages 40–44.

The Attitude of Nonjudgmental Reflection

Reflection is an essential practice if you want to find your way through conflict. You need to be able to reflect on complex situations, your role in them, and the feelings and sensations that arise in your body when you live through and recall them. The attitude of nonjudgmental reflection is listed first to highlight the importance of developing the ability—the attitude—to reflect without judgment on the people involved in your conflict.

Often, for most people, the most challenging nonjudgmental reflection isn't refraining from criticizing others. It's refraining from criticizing and judging themselves. Time and again, we have encountered educators who are quick to point out their own faults, always ready to apologize for and explain all that they've done wrong in any given situation. That's why we think the attitude of nonjudgmental reflection is essential for everyone involved.

The Attitude of Humble Curiosity

Over and over, as our curiosity leads us down some new path, we have our deeply held assumptions overturned and our strong initial conclusions questioned. When we become arrogant, convinced of the accuracy of our positions, we try to pry loose that arrogance with humility. That's a practice that comes with experience: the more we learn about conflict, the more we learn how little we know.

You will find your way through conflict more effectively if you can appreciate your cognitive blind spots. You will engage conflict more effectively if you can take a deep breath and courageously admit your errors.

The Attitude of Self-Effacing Humor

Finding our way through conflict can mean we lose our grip on being an assured professional. There we are, bumbling around at our worst—it doesn't really seem like it would be fun or funny to look at! But if we cut ourselves some slack and realize that our bumbling is what makes us human, we gain a bit of cheerful yet mindful distance from those things.

When we approach our sticky conflicts with some mindfulness, we can admit that we are who we are in the moment, and that the moment is a result of a series of causes and conditions, decisions and choices. We'll never untangle all of those factors, to be sure, and that means we're likely to find ourselves in many of the same situations later no matter how hard we try. Given the absurdity of it all, why not poke a bit of fun at ourselves?

The Attitude of Accepting Imperfection

Practice will never make perfect. Instead, we know that practice gives us more and more opportunities to learn that our goal should be a more thoughtful engagement with the imperfection that is inherent in all conflicts. Thankfully, we have ourselves and others, a bunch of similarly imperfect humans getting into conflicts that lead to imperfect solutions. Now and then we gain a sliver of insight or a newly useful tactic, something that allows us to see that imperfection with a bit more clarity.

That's why we adopt the attitude that practice makes imperfect. Become good at harnessing all the nonjudgmental reflection, humble curiosity, and self-effacing humor you can muster, and engage in each conflict with a commitment to learning from the practice.

The Neurology and Psychology of Stickiness

Here's a little meditative experiment. Find a relatively quiet, subdued place where you can be alone and do nothing. Set a timer for ten minutes, close your eyes or focus on something in your visual field, and do your best to bring awareness to whatever passes through your mind.

As you do, start counting to yourself, one number per breath. If you can, count to ten and then return back to 1. Do that for the full ten minutes.

When the timer goes off, consider the following questions.

Did you notice how hard it was for your brain to attend consistently to the task at hand? For most people, this exercise is impossible; they can't maintain the "simple" counting exercise for a full ten minutes. In fact, many people can't make it to ten, trying over and over again as their frustration grows.

Did you notice what disrupted your counting? For most people, it's nearly impossible to recall it all: shopping lists, the call you have to make to your parents, that work task you're dreading, your editor's pointed question, that silly social media post, an embarrassing moment with your boss . . . You don't know how those intrusive thoughts started or where they went; you didn't actively request their presence. Suddenly, the thoughts or feelings were just there—and just as suddenly they were gone.

Did some of those disruptions get sticky? Did that dreadful work task eat up an anxious minute or two? Did that embarrassing moment with your boss get your stomach churning?

This exercise is a great way to learn a simple fact that most of us don't like very much. It turns out that our brains do things that we don't want or ask them to do. For example, the seemingly random, chattery activity is something brains just do. Brains are like glands that secrete thoughts, which appear suddenly without a beginning and disappear without a trace.

Some of those thoughts are tied to feelings—the anxieties, disappointments, and frustrations that make thoughts linger. Those sticky thoughts have a neurological basis, one that you'll need to understand to find your way through conflict.

There are many models available to understand the neurological research about brains, emotions, and reasoning. We find Dr. Becky Bailey's brain states model to be a very useful, three-part framework for understanding why, exactly, our brains can get us so stuck (Bailey 2015).

Before reading about the brain states model, take a moment to write down a few sentences describing your experiences during each of the following three types of conflict:

- a conflict in which you felt panicky and scared that something truly catastrophic was going to happen to you, even if you weren't sure what that would be

- a conflict in which you feared you would lose the love or appreciation of a partner or colleague if you didn't handle the conflict right

- a conflict in which you felt a calm, reasoned confidence throughout, a sense that you could figure out the problem with relative ease and weren't threatened with the loss of safety or love

Got all three? Let's look at that scary one first.

The Survival State: Am I Safe?

Review your reflection about the panicky, scary conflict. Can you remember what it felt like in your body? Chances are pretty good that, even as you remember it, you are holding your breath, clenching your fists or jaw, or jiggling your knee up and down as you sit.

Can you recall the difficulty you had in sorting out what exactly was happening? Did you notice that your usually perceptive senses focused tightly on one specific thing, or shut down completely? Did your ability to problem-solve disappear without a trace?

Some conflicts are very good at throwing us into this state. We all have emotions that can erase our sense of safety. When this happens, our bodies flood with stress hormones like adrenaline and cortisol. We are in fight, flight, or freeze mode, experiencing an "amygdala hijack" (Goleman 2005, 60–61).

Dr. Bailey and others call this the survival state for good reason. Our brains—like the brains of all other mammals and many other animals—have a built-in switch that activates our defenses to protect us from perceived threats. And thanks to our personal histories and lived experiences, lots of things can trigger that sense of threat—it doesn't take a lion, tiger, or bear!

> When we are in a conflict that has our bodies amped up on stress hormones and our cognitive functioning scuttled, we desperately seek the safest place we can find.

The physical reaction is often easy to recognize, whereas, thanks to amygdala hijacking, the cognitive reaction is hard for us to perceive. It turns out that the amygdala doesn't merely impact our fists and jaws and legs. It also flips several switches in our brains, turning off access to our prefrontal cortex (where we learn and apply reason) and making access to useful memories very difficult.

As a result, when we are in a conflict that has our bodies amped up on stress hormones and our cognitive functioning scuttled, we desperately seek the safest place we can find. That's what makes "I'm right and you're wrong" so sticky in the most challenging conflicts: without access to the tools that grant us logic, insight, and perspective, we retreat into the most defensive position our fear presents. "I need security; you are a threat" is a pretty good translation of that right/wrong duality when your amygdala has taken control.

In this state, as Bailey indicates, there is exactly one question: "Am I safe?" This is the stickiest question of all, the one that you simply cannot shake when your body is coursing with stress and your brain has lost access to reasoning. Every strategy in this book will fail while you're in this state. Your brain has one thought: "You are a threat to me; why would I ever want to connect to you?"

It takes a lot of practice to develop a sense of respect for and understanding about yourself in this state, practice that occurs before and after you're in it, largely. And you'll need help from the other two states to do so.

The Emotional State: Am I Loved?

Think back to the personal conflict you wrote about in chapter 2. As we describe there, most people in our workshops have focused largely on the emotions they experienced in the conflict, rather than focusing on the outcome of the conflict. Emotions were their focus not only during the conflict, but also well after it was over.

That's because there's a lot at stake when we are faced with a difficult moment with another person. Even if we're not worried about a threat to our very existence, the emotional aspect is often the most memorable part of a conflict. It tugs at our identity, our value, and our worth. Even if we feel physically safe, our emotional safety feels tenuous, and we are uncertain as we confront questions about our social and professional place at work. Do I fit in? Can I be myself here? Or, as Dr. Bailey puts it, we wonder: "Am I loved?"

The fearful risk of losing love or appreciation can cause you to get stuck in your feelings, creating big barriers to finding your way through conflict.

At the beginning of this exercise, you wrote down a conflict in which you feared you would lose the love or appreciation of a partner or colleague if you didn't handle the conflict right. Typically, the fearful risk of losing love or appreciation can cause you to get stuck in your feelings, creating big barriers to finding your way through conflict. That's no accident. It's a neurochemical feature of every human brain and body.

Even if we are physically safe, our bodies are still in high alert until we are emotionally safe. The stress hormones like cortisol remain active in our bodies and prevent us from engaging in productive, cognitive thought processes. Things are out of whack; our emotional balance is difficult to maintain. And when that happens, we can't fully and effectively engage in rational discussions.

In conflict, things are even more dicey. As Becky Bailey explains, the only way to soothe big emotions is through connection. Connection with another person allows us to resolve the question of whether we are loved—not necessarily the love we experience in intimate relationships, but more generally the genuine experience of being seen and valued. Of course, when you're feeling vulnerable, the last person you're likely to turn to is your counterpart. That's the paradox: the person whose connection you would most likely benefit from in that moment is the one you feel most distant from and threatened by.

Nevertheless, if you can summon the courage to pursue that connection, all parties will benefit. Validating big emotions calms the emotions and your body, allowing you to return to balance in your brain, to move into a learning state by activating your prefrontal lobe, where the best thinking happens. (We'll talk more about how to do this in the next chapter.)

The Executive State: What Can I Learn?

Our goal in this book is to help you learn how to reach the executive state—a place where you feel safe, secure, and ready to learn, even in the midst of conflict—more regularly. We can't prevent all the feelings; your brain is going to do what brains do. But we can help you understand what gets in the way of being able to reach this state.

A lot is revealed about our identity and emotional footprint in the first two states. However, when our brains are flooded with cortisol, we are less likely to retain new information no matter how powerful it is. When you have clearly established a sense of physical and emotional safety, everything changes. Once stress hormones are balanced and connection is established or re-established, we can engage logic and sort through the conflict, articulating what happened, brainstorming solutions, and working toward a response. For both children and adults, learning and brain development occur when we are in the executive state.

Consider now the third conflict you wrote down in this exercise. You chose it precisely because it is the easiest to think about; all threats to your physical and emotional well-being were quelled. Even if the content of the conflict was difficult, you probably can recall that you approached this conflict by sharing different ideas, discussing concrete details, and considering alternative perspectives to reach a response through genuine give-and-take. These are all indicators that both parties were in the executive brain state.

There's the catch: *both* people need to be safe and connected before anyone can move on to the executive state. It's actually impossible for us to solve a problem until we are calmly, mutually in this thinking space together. Put differently, you'll do a better job of finding your way through conflict if you and your counterpart can, together, co-regulate and thereby help each other feel safe.

Engaging the Observing Self

So, what are you supposed to do with all that brain state information? Dr. Bailey has a tidy demonstration that is very valuable in conflict, one that involves activating what some psychologists call the observing self. Three people stand in a line all facing the same direction. Each person holds a sign to represent the executive state, the emotional state, and the survival state. All three states are looking forward, out toward the world.

Then, Bailey asks the person in the front—representing the executive state—to turn around to face the other two people and to take a step or two backward. This sequence enacts the observing self: the executive state looks at the emotional state and the survival state and asks, "What can I learn?"

It's a simple yet powerful demonstration, one that we use often in our work with our faculty teams and one that we encourage you to use as well. It takes practice; to be able to engage our learning brain in sticky situations, we have to turn that learning brain toward the very neurological elements that shut it down. But once you're good at it, you can ask yourself some powerful questions. What can you see when you turn your observing self toward your brain states? What can you learn about what gets you stuck?

We don't know about you, but, for us, understanding the neurology of stickiness provides a welcome sense of relief about all we bring into conflicts. After all, we are describing what human brains and bodies are built to do. These states have very specific functions that have developed over thousands of years to ensure our species exists. They make evolutionary sense.

And that means that getting stuck is our heritage, connected to basic animal and mammalian neurology, and not some lack of intelligence or character flaw. You are supposed to run from difficult conflict, so give yourself a break.

The Psychology of Stickiness in Conflict

Take a moment to jump on your social media accounts. As you probably already know, your stream of information in those accounts is a carefully calibrated machine for making money. That stream is calculated based on algorithms that will prompt you to use more bandwidth, spend more time, make a few purchases here or there, and, most importantly, click and click again.

Clickbait is built to be sticky. As a result, our social media streams provide good illustrations of some of the foundational principles that help explain psychological stickiness. These principles are particularly easy to see in the ways that social media algorithms encourage us to sustain conflict as an ongoing cultural and political climate.

Let's take a look at your political news feed, for example. Facebook and Twitter algorithms want to "feed" us content that we'll enjoy consuming, and that includes content that aligns with our political views. We'll see positive stories about politicians and policies we admire, and negative stories about those we despise.

Like our brains, these algorithms seek to feed both our logic centers and the rest of our neurology. Content that makes us feel part of something—a community, a culture, a movement—is designed to make us feel safe and loved within it. And just as it does in conflict, that same content can feed our sense of threat. Put differently, your brain is feeding not your logic but your convictions, that stew of insight, perception, "gut feeling," reasoning, and intuition to which, come hell or high water, you are sticking.

In conflict and elsewhere, the algorithm that our brains use to sort the information that is feeding our convictions has a name: confirmation bias. That is, your brain operates as a sorting machine, determining what does and does not confirm your sense of what's right, valuing the former and tossing out the latter (Heshmat 2015).

We desire to see ourselves as having control over our reasoning, regardless of how much time we spent meditating as our mind chatters away. But confirmation bias is a psychological reality, one that is pretty easy to spot if you take the time to do so.

Do you have a relative you see around this or that holiday, someone who supports a candidate or position with whom you disagree? Have you noticed that it is very, very difficult to convince this person that their candidate is a moron, no matter how many courses of Thanksgiving dinner you eat? Did they ignore your most forceful reasoning, and grab onto this or that sentence in order to twist it into a club to prove that they are right and you are wrong?

Oh, one more thing. Did you notice that, no matter how hard they try, they can't overturn your confirmation bias either?

When we're in the midst of those sorts of difficult conversations, in which we're sure that we're right and the other person is wrong, our brain's algorithm sorts the string of information that our opponent presents into two buckets. We might call one "Charlie Brown's teacher," a sort of meaningless "wah wah wah" noise that comes from someone else's mouth but not in the form of sensible words. Our brain ignores that stuff because it's not important to us; whether it's important to the other person doesn't matter.

Meanwhile, when our brain hears something that confirms our biases and convictions, it gives it a big "Aha!" sticker. Suddenly, our brain is paying very close attention, remembering phrases we'll spit back at our counterpart as proof that they're wrong and we're right, phrases that activate not only our cognitive centers but all of our brain states. The "Aha!" content sticks; the rest of it flows unnoticed into the dustbin.

This sort of motivated reasoning leads to confirmation bias, the biggest, stickiest psychological obstacle to finding your way through conflict. Your brain is going to do all it can to hold onto its sense of safety, assert its convictions, and sort for information that will sustain its confirmation bias. In doing so, your brain is working very hard to convince you that a particularly difficult conflict is about much more than a parking space, political candidate, or clerical error.

That's because your brain knows what we keep repeating: every difficult conflict is a conflict about *you*. Stickiness is your brain's most effective strategy for convincing you that your sense of self is at stake. Confirmation bias confirms what your brain needs confirmed—and each item was chosen precisely because it does so. And if it doesn't confirm your bias, well, your brain doesn't need to pay attention to that. "Wah, wah, wah."

Sadly for us all, in conflict, our brains are simply not at their best. Chances are pretty good that large chunks of your brain are offline or operating at less than 100 percent capacity. So your brain is a bit sloppier than you'd like to think it usually is. It's not very articulate. It blurs the big and little pictures; it's focused completely on the moment while paying little attention to what comes next.

Most of all, it wants to convince you that you are right in this moment and you've been right all along. In conflict, your brain wants you to believe that it's got your back, that it's taking your best interests to heart, that it knows what's good for you.

It doesn't. And that's the stickiest thing to unstick.

To find your way through conflict, you have to learn how not to believe your brain in conflict. Here are a few tips.

Practicing with Stickiness

Given that stickiness is our neurological and psychological reality, we need to figure out ways to practice with it. To do so, we rely on our four attitudes of nonjudgmental reflection, humble curiosity, self-effacing humor, and accepting imperfection.

Let's start with the most challenging part.

Distinguish Between Your Thoughts and Reality

It's a sobering realization for most of us. The science is clear: in conflict, our brains are simply not telling us the truth.

So it's important in conflict to learn that your number-one job is to distinguish between your thoughts and reality. Your assessments, interpretations, analyses, all of the cognitive tools that you use to make sense of the world, are compromised. They are *most* compromised when your brain tells you, in loud and demanding tones, "I've got this."

Learning that you can't get unstuck from the stickiness is a long road. And the learning typically occurs in the most challenging situations. You need that nonjudgmental self-reflection to see where you got it wrong—often very wrong—in the heat of the moment. You need that curiosity grounded in humility to pick apart what your brain presented as reality and compare it to what you learned later. And if you can bring some self-effacing humor to these moments, they are a lot easier to endure.

The stickiness of conflict is part of our human heritage. Our neurology and psychology have been shaped to cultivate a secure certainty when in conflict. It's our job to learn ways to counter that certainty and introduce a healthy dose of affable skepticism into the situation.

Lucky for you, one of the easiest tricks is part of the early childhood educator's regular tool kit.

Remember This Key Child Development Principle

Do you remember the time when you were talking to a frustrated colleague new to early childhood education, someone who described a child with phrases like "He's just defiant" or "She's terrible at that!" In those moments, we turn to a very powerful insight that's hard to remember but essential to our field: behavior and identity are not the same.

A toddler who chooses not to comply with your insistence that he clean up his toys is not "just defiant." A preschooler who struggles with counting isn't "terrible at that." Each of those behaviors means something specific. But individual behaviors can never be generalized to describe who a child is.

It's a basic rule of early childhood education, right? Too bad your brain forgets it in conflict.

When you're in the midst of a sticky conflict, your brain is busy convincing you that the missteps, facial expressions, and blurted sentences of your counterpart all add up to more than the sum of their parts. Instead of treating each behavior as if it has its own meaning, your brain generalizes. The behaviors reveal your counterpart's "true colors," showing you who they "really are." You're right; they're wrong. It's all very neat and tidy, isn't it?

Equating behavior and identity is very sticky indeed, and that's when you need to use your early childhood educator skill set. As your brain starts to merge behavior and person, take a step back and reassess. How can you distinguish between the behavior and the person? What might the behavior mean if someone else perceived it, someone whose brain isn't busy confirming its prejudicial bias?

Finally, how might the conflict be creating a lousy environment for that person in the first place? After all, you're certainly not at your best—that's why you're taking the backward step. So how about lending a little grace to your counterpart and assuming that, just maybe, they are not at their best either?

Honor the Power of Ambivalence

If you're like most people, you're probably not sure you want to commit to such grace. You likely see some of the benefits of changing your attitude—but just as quickly you can feel the pull of sustaining your convictions.

That is to say, you're ambivalent about making such a change in your attitude, your approach, your perspective. That lack of conviction to truly overcome our biases has had the sustained attention of researchers into behavior and change. As William Miller and Stephen Rollnick put it in their excellent book, *Motivational Interviewing: Helping People Change*, "Ambivalence is simultaneously wanting and not wanting something, or wanting both of two incompatible things. It has been human nature since the dawn of time" (Miller and Rollnick 2013, 6). As you can imagine, ambivalence is sticky: if it weren't, you'd set it aside and do the right thing with those cigarettes, candy bars, and glasses of wine, right?

The process of motivational interviewing that Miller and Rollnick describe in their book turns toward, not away from, that sticky ambivalence. In doing so, they identify two types of talk that are mixed together in the stories people tell about themselves when they are considering a shift in behavior.

One type is sustain talk, "a person's own arguments for not changing, for sustaining the status quo" (Miller and Rollnick 2013, 7). This is what your brain does in conflict, producing a stream of sustain talk about the vice, the conflict, your counterpart, the legitimacy of your perspective, and so on. It's perfectly normal for your brain to do this, of course, but ambivalence means that there's something else afoot.

That something else is revealed by change talk, "the person's own statements that favor change" (Miller and Rollnick 2013, 7). In conflict, you want to listen for those brief moments of change talk, and you can evoke them with a few simple questions that poke holes in the sustain talk.

- Is there another way to think about this situation?

- What are some other possible explanations?

- Do I want to get out of this conflict instead of perpetuating it?

Developing a healthy appreciation for sustain talk means that you can start noticing when it crops up and labeling it as such. When you notice that sustain thinking, you can prompt yourself to consider some change thinking. All the while, remember the attitude of nonjudgmental reflection and humble curiosity: you're just human, after all, but there's something interesting happening and you should take a look at it.

Know What You Can and Can't Control

Let's add one more way that humans get stuck: our innate desire for control.

A great deal of being an early childhood educator involves control and planning: staffing to remain in ratio; coordinating children's biological routines; implementing a consistent schedule with engaging experiences for young children; planning curriculum and assessments. These sorts of controls help our children thrive and keep programs running efficiently. But in conflict, our need for control can trip us up. We can get stuck on things we can't change, spinning around powerlessly while complaining about the power we don't have. Meanwhile, we can overlook the very things we have the power to change. And we often struggle to find the line between those two categories.

Here's an exercise to help you get unstuck from your desire to have control and stop getting stuck on things out of your control. The goal is to develop strong change language that echoes the strategies above about motivation and ambivalence.

In the middle of a sheet of paper, draw a circle and label it "Things I/we can change." Label the outside space "Things I/we can't change." This diagram provides a strong visual reminder of what you can and can't control.

Now carefully consider the factors relevant to a conflict you're in or a problem you're trying to solve. Think about where to place each item—can you change it or can't you? Write it in the appropriate place. If you're working with others, discuss this with them too. It may take a bit of time to come up with all the small and large details contributing to your situation, so give it some thought.

Here's a diagram that Chris created in his program:

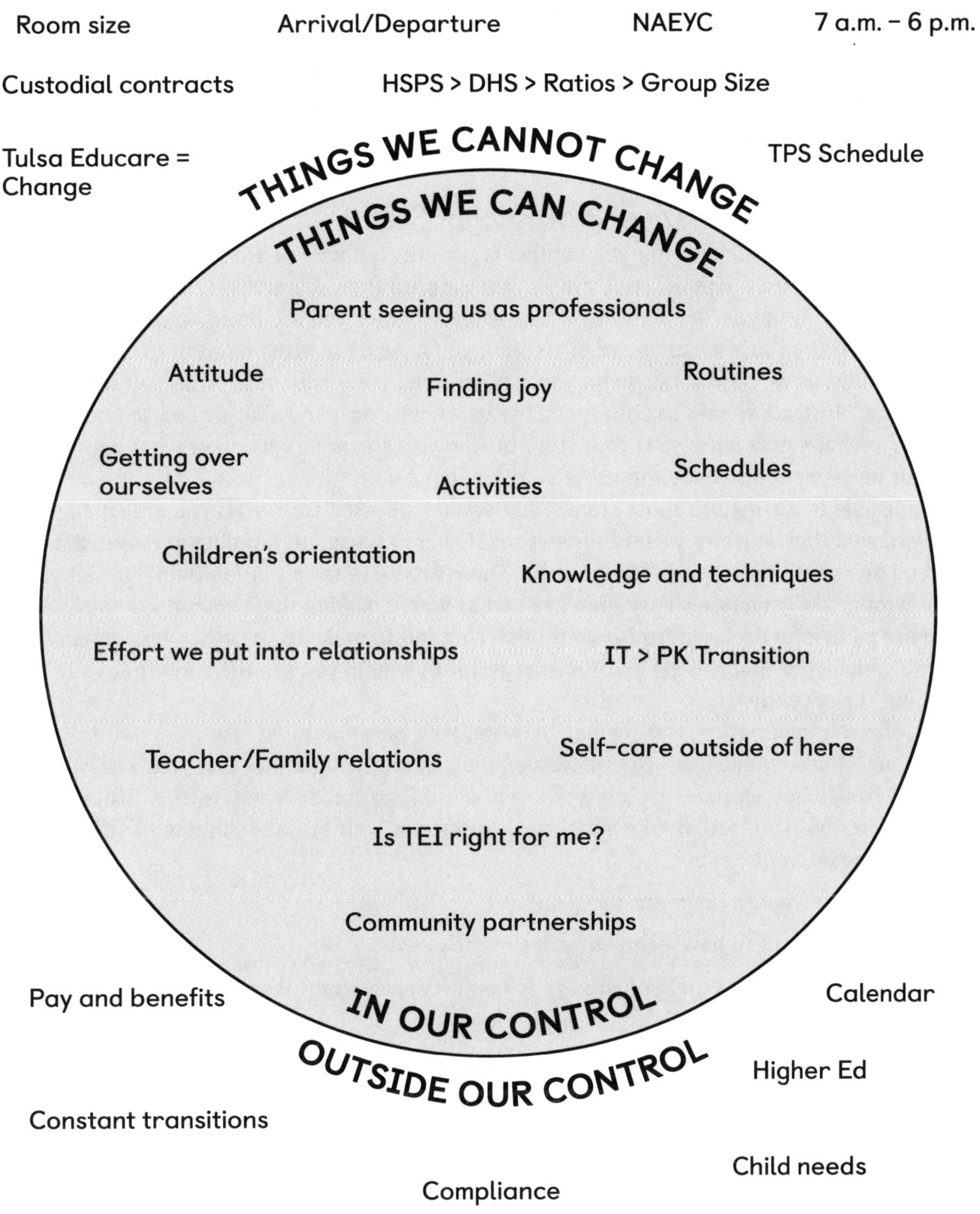

Room size   Arrival/Departure   NAEYC   7 a.m. – 6 p.m.

Custodial contracts   HSPS > DHS > Ratios > Group Size

Tulsa Educare = Change   TPS Schedule

THINGS WE CANNOT CHANGE

THINGS WE CAN CHANGE

Parent seeing us as professionals

Attitude   Finding joy   Routines

Getting over ourselves   Activities   Schedules

Children's orientation   Knowledge and techniques

Effort we put into relationships   IT > PK Transition

Teacher/Family relations   Self-care outside of here

Is TEI right for me?

Community partnerships

Pay and benefits   **IN OUR CONTROL**   Calendar

OUTSIDE OUR CONTROL   Higher Ed

Constant transitions

Child needs

Compliance

Considering and placing each item in its proper space can be a cathartic problem-solving experience. When effective, it is empowering, loosening the sticky things outside our control, creating a framework that reflects reality, and focusing our attention on the areas where our efforts can have an impact. Over time, additional conversations may reveal that some things you thought were outside of your control actually can be impacted by your efforts—a very empowering moment indeed.

Activating the Observing, Professional Self

By now it's clear: the stickiest thing in conflict is you! In conflict you are seeking to defend your perspectives, your actions, your values—all the stuff that, if you add it up, makes you "you." And given your tendency to worry about whether you are loved, appreciated, respected, and even safe when you're in conflict, you have a big investment in that "you."

Thankfully, as we now know, "who you are" isn't the same person as "who you tell yourself you are." Instead, thanks to your fears, biases, convictions, and sharply focused narratives in conflict, what you're stuck to is your story of who you are, your version of what happened, and your investment in the legitimacy of your feelings.

Being able to distinguish those stories that you tell yourself from who you are enables a backward step that activates your observing self. "There I go again, jumping to conclusions based on one or two missteps;" "Caught you! There's more to the situation than 'I'm right and you're wrong;'" "C'mon now! They aren't as bad as you're making them sound, are they?" These are all helpful declarations for your observing self to make to the other, less observant self into which your brain keeps pouring energy, for they help you see the ways that your brain misfires in conflict.

In reflective supervision, this by-play between your observant and less observant selves has a name. When you activate your *professional use of self*, you neither toss your sticky self into the garbage nor accept every story that self is trying to convince you is true. Instead, you ask your observant self to take a look at those stories your brain is clinging to and think through some other questions.

- Who do you want to be in this moment?

- Who do you want to have been when it's over?

- Your position requires that you engage in conflict successfully. What parts of you do you need to activate to do this?

- What's sticky for you here? Where are you making misplaced investments in this situation?

- Where are you clinging to sustain behavior instead of change behavior?

Remember Christine's story from chapter 1 about staffing at her center and the shame she can feel in a difficult week? It turns out that her staff felt that she handled that week incredibly well—they lined up to tell her that on the following Monday.

And that's because Christine was able to distinguish between herself and her professional use of that self. Her emotions were real, to be sure, but she was able to use her observing self to take a good look at that shame and keep it in check while getting through her difficult days. Neither denying those emotions nor indulging them, Christine was able to authentically enact her professional self.

The only way that this can work is if you ask those questions above in the spirit of our four attitudes. You have to be able to look at your not-very-professional self without getting too judgmental about it, and that takes practice. You need to find the self-reflective sweet spot that allows you to admit that this perspective or that interpretation isn't helping your professional self very much, while at the same time identifying that its flaws are not indicators of your failure as a person.

Instead, you need to find ways to mine your imperfect self for insights that your humble curiosity has identified. And, if you're able, it's good to chuckle now and then. Chances are pretty good that you've seen these blemishes quite a few times before and, given your brain's ambivalence, you're having a hard time giving them up.

Remember: Accept Imperfection

In every conflict, you have to balance solving the particular conflict that you're in and learning how to find your way through conflict with that person in general. While we like to believe that practice makes perfect, in conflict, practice makes imperfect. There's no goal line or measure of being "good" at conflict.

At any given moment, you might find you can't come up with the "fix" for that situation. But that result isn't failure. Chances are you made some progress in figuring out how to be in conflict, how to be in a more productive, authentic relationship with your counterpart, and how to be who you truly are in that relationship and those conflicts. To do this, we have to engage, fully and humbly, without sticking to the idea of perfection or resolution.

Christine's sticky kid is a good example of that sort of engagement. His challenging behavior has lingered with her for decades because it was unresolved.

I think about this child all the time. Of course, I wish we had reached a resolution, a happy ending, an outcome that promised him future success. That's the lousy part of the stickiness.

But there's a productive part of the stickiness too. I regularly think about the perseverance the adults in his life possessed to be able to consider every angle of support for that child. Each time I'm faced with a difficult situation with a child, I remember that I don't know how to be perfect in it—but I learned a lot about being imperfect in it.

Fast-forward many years. Once again, I had a child who exhibited big, challenging behaviors in the classroom. My role was to provide support to the teachers when things had escalated beyond their range of expertise. The first time I met this child, he was in a full-blown demonstration of his power and unraveled self-regulation. He was throwing toys, dumping bins, yelling, and flipping furniture.

In these situations, early childhood educators want to know the magic formula for prevention and intervention. But if this scenario sounds at all familiar to you, you know the painful reality: children don't come with a magic wand or a user's manual.

The only magic I bring to this are my years of imperfections, humility, and reflection. I remember thinking, "I don't know how this is going to end but I remember how to be imperfect in it." From my first sticky child years before, I knew how to be in the moment. How to see *him*. How to trust myself to connect with him.

I remembered how to just *be*. I sat down. I paused to remember what trust looks like, so I took a big breath and relaxed my shoulders. I remembered the importance of being neutral and objective, so I said, "Wow, there are a lot of things out of place." I remembered what it means to be seen without judgment, so I said, "Things got big. And loud. Whew."

He stopped throwing things. He stopped yelling. And we picked up the toys together.

Sounds magical, right? It wasn't magical, or speedy, or tidy, I assure you. And this wasn't the last time that this child exhibited difficult behavior.

But it was our first moment of connection. Each time I had to jump in and support him, that real connection we shared set the tone for our interactions. I was committed to bringing all of me and really showing up to be with him in the moment every time things got big. Slowly, gradually, we saw real progress.

Imperfect. But with humility, reflection, and a commitment to be a little more present each time, you create a chance to activate what you learned in previous situations.

Even when a situation is resolved, it doesn't guarantee success in all future conflict situations. We have to keep showing up with the reflection, humility, and curiosity that allow for growth. And this means offering that grace to other people too, adults and children alike. Remembering your imperfection can help you make space for the imperfection of others. Let people recover and come back. Let them try again. Let them get better at working through conflicts. Otherwise we eliminate the possibility of growth and success.

CHAPTER 4

PRACTICE MAKES IMPERFECT

Since we can't work at being in conflict without the presence of conflict—and we certainly don't want you to go out and create one—we need good, strong situations in which to practice. This chapter focuses on case studies about conflict between two fictional characters, Robin and Pat, who provide a lot for us to learn from. Their nuanced conflicts include sticky perspectives that could produce a strong investment from you in the outcome. If you're reading this book with colleagues or would like to go through the case studies with folks at work, use the downloadable PLC guide, found at freesprit.com/PLC.

As you read the chapter, you'll see reflective questions after many sections. We hope that you'll use them to think again about the conflicts from your life and work that you've pondered so far.

We have learned that the experience of role playing provides a powerful experience for workshop participants, and we believe the same will be true for you. Some lessons about conflict cannot be explained. They must be felt. And the feelings are likely to be many and powerful, both odd and predictable. Big feelings can be overwhelming, so before you act on any temptation to skip over this chapter and avoid said feelings, let's explore why working through big emotions is crucial.

Every Difficult Conversation Is a Three-In-One

In most conflict resolution trainings, emotions are one part of a multi-step process for working through conflict. While there are many versions of conflict resolution ranging from three steps to nine steps, those carefully scripted steps can be sorted into two basic parts: what happened and what people felt.

In the first part, the "what happened" stage, participants are expected to recall, as simply as possible, the objective components of the event in question. We refer to this exploration as *looping*, in which you inquire what happened, repeat back what someone said, and acknowledge its legitimacy. We talk more about that in chapter 7.

The second part involves the exploration of each person's feelings. The speaker uses "I feel" statements, and the listener expresses empathy for those declarations of emotion, after which the roles are reversed. Put together, the two parts offer what seems to be a simple, clear way to resolve conflict.

The problem is that the two-part process rarely works. Here's why.

As we've discussed earlier, it is hard to do otherwise simple things like separating "what happened" and "feelings" during a difficult conversation. Our brains yank us back into reactivity, and we experience again the sticky emotions and sensations that are evoked by the situation we're trying to describe. In addition, it's a challenging cognitive task to order your reactivity properly, sequencing what happened first and how you felt about it second.

It takes a lot of practice to untangle our jumbled reactions, with feelings seeping into our descriptions of events. Plus, it requires a lot of self-awareness to recognize all of the complicated investments we have in what details we select and emphasize, how we reach our judgments, and so on.

When we have big feelings, our brains just aren't good at careful, distanced analysis, and as a result what comes out of our mouths is more often than not an emotional mishmash. Often tied up in this are blame, accusations, and deflection of our contributions. If you've ever been on the receiving end of blame, you know that it usually results in escalated tension, not in resolution.

So if you've tried resolving conflict using only these two parts, you know the conflict likely remains unresolved. There always seems to be something else floating around besides the event itself and our feelings about it. Here's a very simple, common household conflict as an example: You're doing your Sunday chores. As you walk down the hall with the week's dirty laundry in a hamper, you spy your partner's used underwear on the floor. Bending down to pick it up, you tip over the hamper, spilling more items on the floor. As you scoop everything up, you realize that you are furious.

Let's apply the two-step process, shall we? What's the event? While you were doing laundry, you noticed that your partner left underwear on the floor—pretty simple stuff. How about the feelings? Maybe it started with some "Here we go again" annoyance you didn't notice, escalated into frustration as you bent over to pick up the item, and exploded into fury after spilling the rest of the laundry.

Feel better? Do you think the conflict would be resolved if you shared those things with your partner?

Something is missing, isn't it? The whole episode is important—but it's "just laundry!" What do we make of that discrepancy? Why, exactly, do you feel that way about a pair of underwear on the floor?

The researchers at the Harvard Negotiation Project decided to identify that missing piece. They had facilitated negotiations involving everything from minor workplace conflicts between two employees to nation-states establishing peace treaties. Across all of those situations, they found a third crucial, ever-present component: identity (Stone, Patton, and Heen 1999).

Let's go back to the underwear on the floor. Every partner has blind spots, bad habits, and other mildly annoying traits: gas tank indicators that too often have the "E" light flashing; poorly loaded dishwashers; missed anniversaries.

But certain traits carry more power than others. Stone, Patten, and Heen make the point—and we heartily agree—that the dirty underwear implicates your identity within the relationship you have with your partner. Like a poorly loaded dishwasher or empty gas tank, that pair of underwear sitting on the floor is a piece of evidence about your identity.

To your brain, that piece of underwear means that, to your partner, you're not a respected member of the household. Instead, that underwear means that you are just a laborer in service to them. That underwear is a marker of disrespect for the work that you do each week for the household, a sign that this work, and therefore you, are unnoticed, invisible, unvalued.

It's not "just underwear." It's more than "just underwear" because, in fact, it's not about under-wear. It's about you, about your identity within your relationship.

> Every conflict is a three-in-one. Our sense of what happened, our feelings about it, and our sense of identity are all simmered together in one messy stew.

Think back to Chris and Christine's conflicts in chapter 2. The family engagement mess that Chris created wasn't, in the end, a catastrophe, and problems like that are a routine occurrence for most school directors. But in that conflict, Chris's identity was under threat: his management of his leadership team, his interactions with tricky parents and guardians, and—perhaps above all!—his expertise in facilitating conflict were at stake. Same for Christine: the schedule proposed by the stand-in program director would've worked just fine. Christine's identity was challenged when her experience and perspective weren't taken into consideration.

We firmly believe that Stone, Patton, and Heen are right: every conflict is a three-in-one. Our sense of what happened, our feelings about it, and our sense of identity are all simmered together in one messy stew. Focusing only on what happened and our related feelings leaves out the most important part, the gas that makes the engine of conflict run. Finding our way through conflict requires that we disentangle those components—and that means we need practice with personal experiences that activate all three of them.

Which brings us to Robin and Pat.

Why Robin and Pat?

More than a decade ago, Chris was asked by a community-based nonprofit agency to help them sort out some concerns that had arisen in their team. He had worked with them before on issues of culture, diversity, and equity, but they continued to struggle when confronting a string of interpersonal conflicts. That fraught struggle presented a challenge: the team lacked the trust needed to dive into a workshop about conflict that engaged specific squabbles, but a workshop that avoided the issues embedded in those squabbles wouldn't be valuable.

So Chris created two characters, Robin and Pat. These two characters have a lot of conflict on issues of culture, diversity, and equity. Over the years, we have revised and refined these two case studies, carefully tweaking the details now and then to make them as effective as possible for our workshop participants.

We've now used Robin and Pat with thousands of workshop participants, to tremendous effect. Without question, it's the most engaging, fun, bizarre, and emotionally powerful part of the workshop, time and again. And while we won't team you up with a partner here in the book (though the PLC guide provides support for doing so), we hope that you'll find the rest of the chapter just as engaging, fun, bizarre, and powerful.

Robin's Case Study

First, we introduce you to Robin. Please read and reread the case study carefully before moving on, as we encourage you to do all you can to inhabit Robin's perspective. While it may seem paradoxical, we assure you that taking on the role of Robin will help you reflect upon your own identity in this conflict scenario, and thus your personal perspective, assumptions, and blind spots—all critical components of the rest of the chapter. So we encourage you to dive into the role with gusto!

Meet Robin

From the beginning of your work together, you just haven't seemed to get along with Pat.

Most of the time when you contribute to a group discussion, Pat leans back in the chair and looks at the ceiling. It makes you feel like Pat just doesn't care about what you're saying and is bored. You have tried to be attentive to Pat in discussions, even enthusiastic, but every time Pat just looks pissed off.

You are also getting the feeling that Pat's annoyance at you is having an effect on your work with other people, and it's frustrating. You aren't from this area, where Pat grew up, so you've had to work hard to reach out to families here. As far as you can tell, Pat hasn't supported that effort at all. Instead, Pat seems to find ways to make you look bad. For example, when you are trying to interact with the families, just when it seems to be starting to work, Pat comes over and dominates the discussion.

Two weeks ago, you considered going to the director to talk with them about the problems between you and Pat. You feel pretty comfortable with the director and raise issues like this regularly. However, just before you did, you heard Pat telling the director that things were going great between the two of you while wearing a big smile! You're convinced that Pat doesn't even think a problem exists, so you decided just to try to forget about it.

Yesterday, you noticed Pat talking to a mother holding her infant about some governmental forms you understand really well thanks to a previous job, and you walked over to help them all out, explaining the appropriate language for them. But when you were helping, Pat got angry and stormed off.

You think it's pretty obvious that Pat has a big problem with you—you were just lending a hand, for crying out loud—so now you feel like you need to get Pat to deal with these issues.

Exploring Robin's Perspective

Now that you've had a chance to get to know Robin, and before exploring Robin's perspective, take a few minutes to consider these questions:

- Who is the "you" that you've brought to Robin's situation?

- Where do you agree with Robin's take? Does Robin's story make sense to you?

- What assumptions are you making about what happened? What pieces are you adding to complete the picture?

- Did any of Robin's reactions prompt a reaction in you? Did Robin's emotions evoke any of your own?

- Finally, if you do indeed identify with Robin in certain ways, who is your "Pat"? And where, specifically, did that Pat come from?

It's time to engage even deeper. Let's explore Robin's perspective.

First, we learn about how things unfold during group meetings. Robin seems to contribute with ease, but, as far as Robin can tell, Pat doesn't even care about those contributions and seems disengaged during those moments.

Next, Robin reveals all the hard work that they've put into supporting the families in the community, a community where Pat, but not Robin, was raised. Not only does Pat fail to help Robin out; Pat seems actively to be undermining Robin, dominating interactions with families.

It's gotten so bad that Robin considers approaching the director, whom Robin feels comfortable with, about the situation. But, given Pat's smiling affirmation, it seems to Robin like a waste of time. Nevertheless, everything comes to a head when Robin contributes support to a family to whom Pat is talking, causing Pat to leave in a huff and leaving Robin frustrated.

It's pretty clear that Robin has grown deeply troubled by the situation with Pat, and that Robin has little trust about working through it. A careful reading of the case study helps us understand why the situation evokes those responses in Robin, all of which are related to identity.

Like most of us working in early childhood, Robin has chosen this profession to be a helpful support to others. Indeed, Robin's identity is tied to doing good—and doing good well. When talking about participation in group discussions, Robin refers to "contributions"; Robin brings experience from previous jobs to this one; Robin has built a comfortable relationship with the director; Robin worked hard to connect to this new community.

Does Robin's perspective feel convincingly sticky? Are you starting to notice some of the blind spots—so common to conflicts—that are preventing Robin from perceiving the situation with greater insight? Let's break down Robin's story using some of the concepts we've explored so far in the book.

Some Key Reflections

First, let's look at how Robin defines conflict. Robin feels that there have been repeated instances in which Pat has either failed to perceive all of the good intentions behind Robin's efforts or has reacted negatively to them. For Robin, it's as if the two are unable to collaborate in their work with families—as if they don't even share the same values.

But is that true? Where, exactly, does Robin turn for evidence of this major difference?

Many of Robin's conclusions come from nonverbal behaviors. Pat looks at the ceiling when Robin talks; Pat's facial expressions demonstrate frustration to Robin. Meanwhile, when Pat does respond to the director's query about how things are going between the two of them, Robin interprets that "Great!" on face value, taking it to mean that Pat sees no conflict between them.

What about the interactions with parents? Did you notice anything interesting about who gets to define which efforts with families are helpful contributions and which efforts are rude disruptions? On the one hand, as Robin sees it, Pat's interactions with families are disruptive to Robin's work with them, proving that Pat doesn't respect that work. However, when Robin steps into one of Pat's interactions with a family, it's proof that Robin is helpful and considerate, not disruptive.

That discrepancy suggests a fundamental lack of trust between Robin and Pat. In addition, Robin's interpretation of Pat's behaviors makes several big assumptions about the meanings of those behaviors, the values that drive them, and the relationship the two of them have—all the complex issues below the surface of the conflict iceberg from chapter 1. Whenever possible, it seems, Robin interprets Pat's actions through that judgmental, suspicious lens.

In that manner, Robin has failed to embrace several of the core principles we discussed in the introduction. Robin is stuck in right/wrong thinking, and it's clear to them who's in the wrong. Indeed, the entire story reads like a lawyer's statement in court determined to blame Pat for the entire situation and absolve Robin from any blame whatsoever. Instead of recognizing that this conflict is reciprocal and therefore exploring contributions, Robin is stacking up evidence for the case against Pat. And Robin doesn't believe the conflict has anything to teach: it's merely a distraction from the work, not the work itself.

Now take a look at Robin's case using the reflection questions from chapter 2.

1. **Whose perspective** did your words reflect the most: yours or the other person's?

2. In your transcription of the conflict, did you spend more time on the **emotional** experience of the conflict or how it ended, the **outcome**?

3. Did you spend more time on **intent** or **impact**?

4. Think back to the conflict itself, what was your comfort level with the tension? Were you fully **immersed in** the moment of conflict or **hurrying to get out** of it?

Is Robin focused on the emotional experience, the situation, or moving toward an outcome? Does Robin have any interest in being in the conflict, acknowledging the rupture, and moving toward repair, or does Robin just want to avoid being in it at all costs?

The most important reflection question for Robin's situation, we think, is the third one, on intent versus impact. Like most of us trying to justify our actions in a difficult situation, Robin repeatedly emphasizes good intentions: contributions, efforts, helping out. In so doing, Robin seems unable or unwilling to explore the impact of those well-intentioned actions. And taking up Pat's perspective isn't part of the path forward for Robin.

But it is for us. Ready to meet Pat?

Pat's Case Study

As you step into Pat's take on the situation, we want to remind you once again of some of our core principles. First and foremost, if you found yourself nodding in agreement as you read Robin's story, you are very likely to find Pat's story unconvincing. Yes, even if it's not "your" conflict, you bring yourself to the role-playing exercise in this chapter, and you may indeed seek to maintain your commitment to Robin's tale by resisting Pat's.

If you think that may apply to you, then Robin's take must somehow implicate certain aspects of your own identity. Even though Robin is an entirely fictional character, Robin's perspective has become sticky for you.

So if that's the case, take a few moments, and a few breaths, before immersing yourself in Pat's perspective.

Meet Pat

From the beginning of your work together, you just haven't seemed to get along with Robin.

You try to listen carefully and focus whenever Robin speaks in meetings, but often Robin talks a lot and doesn't allow others to join in. When you can finally get a word in, Robin doesn't seem to listen at all. Sometimes Robin even starts a conversation with the person sitting in the next chair when you are talking.

It hasn't been a big deal until recently. Sure, it was annoying when you'd try to help when Robin was struggling to communicate with a family (usually Robin would act frustrated when you did that). After all, you love to work with the families here in the town where you grew up, and you know that they value your efforts—they tell you every day. It didn't matter that Robin didn't get it; Robin grew up somewhere else but came here for college. It's your community, but not really Robin's community.

However, Robin seems very tight with the director, who's also not from around here, and they chat all the time. You've never been that comfortable with the director, and you certainly wouldn't bring issues like this up. Who knows what the boss would think about you if you complained? The other day, when the director and Robin were talking, the director saw you and asked you how things were going—but the director asked in that "I don't really mean it" way, so you smiled and said fine.

Yesterday, you were talking to a mother you know well when Robin walked up and just interrupted you. When you tried to participate again, Robin jumped in again and corrected your language.

Now you're really frustrated: you won't stand to have someone disrespect you in front of the families in your community. It's time to get Robin to deal with these issues.

Exploring Pat's Perspective

If Robin and Pat have done what we've asked them to do in this book, you should be nodding, exclaiming, "Ohhh!" and smiling.

That has been the reaction for our workshop participants over the years: as they swap roles and read the other person's story, it's as if a dozen doors that had been closed fly open all at once, letting in more light and warmth and air. Suddenly Robin is a flesh-and-blood person, vulnerable and flawed, not an easily judged jerk; suddenly Pat is a human, not a caricature, working on a different set of vulnerabilities and flaws.

Once again, we encourage you to take a few minutes to consider this set of questions, tweaked slightly from those above:

- Who is the "you" that you've brought to Pat's situation?

- Where do you agree with Pat's take? Does Pat's story "make sense"?

- What additional assumptions did you discover you were making about what happened? What pieces were you adding to complete the picture?

- Did any of Pat's reactions prompt a reaction in you? Did Pat's emotions evoke any of your own?

- Finally, if you do indeed identify with Pat in certain ways, who is your "Robin"? And where, specifically did that Robin come from?

Conflict constrains meaning by erasing nuance and complexity, so we want to devote a lot of time and attention to those nuances and that complexity.

> Conflict constrains meaning by erasing nuance and complexity, so we want to devote a lot of time and attention to those nuances and that complexity.

Let's start with one of the simplest yet most nuanced parts of the two case studies: listening. Robin is convinced that Pat isn't listening because Pat stares at the ceiling; Pat is convinced Robin isn't listening because Robin starts conversations with others. Yet both claim to be listening. What's going on here?

Remember: we typically adopt the behaviors that our cultures teach us as the norm, and we attribute meanings and values to those norms. Then, in conflict, when someone behaves in a manner that is not aligned with our norm, that behavior becomes proof that our sticky, judgmental perspective is right.

Listening is a perfect example. For some people, attentive listening means sitting still, making eye contact with the speaker, and gesturing with nods and smiles to demonstrate your attention. Neither Robin nor Pat does this—and thus each judges the other not to be listening.

But these stories make it clear that, in order to focus, Pat looks up while Robin is talking, a very common form of attentive listening in which a person removes distractions from their visual field so they can focus on what they are hearing.

Try it now: look up at the ceiling and see if it helps you to listen more attentively to the ambient sound in the room. What do you now hear that you didn't a few moments ago when you were taking in and processing the words on the page?

What about Robin? Instead of seeking individually focused attention like Pat, some people listen in dialogue with another listener. It happens all the time in our workshops: a participant turns to another with excitement to repeat or expand upon an idea we've just shared. They're not distracted; they are deeply engaged, driven to act by that engagement. So, given the stories you've read, is it any surprise that Robin talks in order to understand?

Both Robin and Pat believe they have demonstrated that they are being extremely attentive listeners, engaging their counterpart's ideas with interest and respect. But because those listening behaviors do not conform to the norms that they are used to individually, the exact opposite happens, and their behaviors feed the other's negative judgment.

More behaviors float through the situation with subtly harmful effect. Take, for example, the two individuals' relationships with the director. Robin understands interactions with the director to be no big deal; Robin finds their relationship comfortable and seems to assume that this comfort is therefore available to everyone on the team.

For Pat, however, the impact of Robin's relationship with the director is very complicated. Unlike Robin, Pat does not feel that sense of comfort; if anything, Pat worries that the director demonstrates a lack of genuine concern. Not only does that mean that Pat is unlikely to "complain" to the director. It also means that, when the director asks how things are going between Pat and Robin, Pat neither takes that as a trustworthy question nor feels safe to provide a truthful response.

> Reflecting on intent versus impact almost always creates a beneficial shift in perspective.

In these stories, the role that the director plays helps us see how supervisory power can flow through a conflict in complex, often hidden ways. Robin and the director share the sort of comfortable relationship that, to Pat, resembles favoritism. The two share a communication style, whereas Pat does not; the two are from outside the community in which they work, whereas Pat grew up here.

Again, while neither the director nor Robin seem to intend to create this sense of favoritism, the impact on Pat is clear. Why risk your position at work by complaining about the apple of your boss's eye? So Pat smiles and then—as we surely have all done more times than we can count—says that everything is fine.

In addition, both Robin and Pat report that they have done all they can to help and support the other person. But "help" and "support," as our two friends indicate, are complicated gestures.

Key Reflections Revisited

In a pattern that repeats itself throughout so many conflicts we see, Pat defines the conflict with Robin by selecting elements that conform to a sense that Robin is utterly to blame for the mess. But notice how remarkably their evidence categories align. Robin doesn't listen (like Pat); Robin interrupts (like Pat); Robin needs help (like Pat); Robin doesn't want to fix the problem (like Pat). In so many ways, their definitions of conflict are mirror images—and rely on decidedly distorted images of each other.

Put differently, Pat echoes Robin's fundamental lack of trust in the relationship. In doing so, Pat leaps quickly from behavior to meaning to values to relationship, never pausing to ask what, exactly, any of those things might mean to Robin. As a result, like Robin, Pat crashes on the iceberg of conflict, hellbent on blame and right/wrong thinking, preferring sticky assumptions to open-minded inquiry.

For us, the key lesson to learn from this conflict is this: reflecting on intent versus impact almost always creates a beneficial shift in perspective. Both Robin and Pat do things intended to help that have negative impacts; both get stuck on their legitimately fine commitments to serve the community, blinding them from the pickles those commitments create. Though the story is fictional, the two of us admit to a deep desire to jump in, grab them both, and say, "Listen up you two. Your focus on why you did what you did is preventing you from seeing the effects of what you did—effects that are easy to fix."

Learning from Robin and Pat

Have you ever been in a conflict in which someone repeatedly insists that they did the very thing that is troubling you "to help"? Often, your counterpart defensively lists a long chain of assumptions that lead to that action, one that's similar to Chris's approach to the frustrated parent back in chapter 2. They perceived a problem or challenge; they determined that the individual dealing with that situation lacks some important thing to solve it; and, as luck would have it, the very thing that you lack is something that they have.

We early childhood educators would decry this sort of deficit-based thinking if it were applied to a child. Instead, with children, we look for strengths, identify opportunities for those strengths to grow and extend to other contexts, and use those strengths as the foundation for other areas of development. However, with adults, we often don't even recognize that we're approaching a situation through that deficit lens, in large part because we're too busy trying to be "helpful."

But the most damaging impact of this "help" to the current mess under consideration is that, unlike Chris with the frustrated parent, both Robin and Pat are lone actors. They rely upon their own perspective; they make judgments based on information gained in that limited perspective; they determine without consulting anyone that they are the solution to the problem—and all of their thinking is based on an initial assumption that the other person lacks the skill, perspective, or insight that they have.

Over and over again, we discover conflicts that grow from precisely this situation. Instead of collaborating in each stage, individuals leap in with their own needs, biases, and perspectives unchecked, their enthusiastic intent blinding them to the impact of their actions. Imagine if, after the first time either had "helped" with a parent, Robin or Pat had simply said to the other, "Can we sit down together and figure out how to do that better?" That simple invitation to dialogue is often enough to avoid all manner of conflicts.

Finally, this notion of "helping" becomes even more complicated when we ask who, exactly, Robin and Pat are there to help. Pat has chosen to do this work in order to serve the community, one that is not Robin's, and receives affirmation from that community regularly. Robin understands and to a degree accepts this outsider designation, a designation that both marginalizes Robin from the community and aligns Robin with the director. As a result, instead of finding a way to align their values regarding their service to the community, these distinctions become, again, the basis upon which the other can be judged. And who suffers due to their lack of collaboration and perspective-taking?

Here are some useful tips to take away from this messy, fascinating conflict.

Consider Possibilities Between Right and Wrong

Like a powerful magnet that pulls us ever forward, right and wrong thinking is almost always a potent, destructive part of conflict. Robin and Pat can't resist the pull, allowing themselves to be drawn into right/wrong thinking as if it is a solution to the situation and not the problem itself. The moral certainty, the stacking of evidence of guilt, the relentless conviction of blame: it's all based on the presupposition that, in a given situation, there is a right and a wrong.

The two of us certainly fall for this all the time, and we suspect that you do as well. But what would happen if, instead of asserting we're right and our counterpart is wrong, we spent some time in the gap between the two? Certainly Robin and Pat would benefit if they recognized that the parents with whom they work come in all shapes and sizes; supporting them requires a sense of nuance, a broad tool kit, and flexibility of perspective. And is it really so terrible if, once in a while, one of them makes a mistake? It's inevitable, a sign of humanity, and not a moral failing.

Explore Whether Both Sides Are "Right"

All too often we meet super-nice early childhood folks who, over and over, find themselves acquiescing in conflicts by setting aside their perspectives, feelings, and agency. That's not conflict resolution—that's surrender! In chapter 7, we spell out how to engage in your conflict resolution discussion, and we urge you to own your story.

Being able to listen, repeat, and acknowledge the other person's story with care and humility opens you up to the realization that, like you, they are simply trying to figure out how to do this complicated work.

That's what we mean here when we say that both sides are "right." Robin's story is an absolutely legitimate perspective on the reality shared with Pat; Pat's story interprets the events that unfold with Robin with the same level of clarity and integrity. One of the key points of this exercise is to recognize that, as so often happens when early childhood educators are in conflict with each other, both parties are doing their level best to manage situations with strong values, deep commitment, and valid intentions.

It's our trust in this insight that makes us such devoted advocates of looping. Being able to listen, repeat, and acknowledge the other person's story with care and humility opens you up to the realization that, like you, they are simply trying to figure out how to do this complicated work doing their best with what they know and see. As a result, simply considering that the other person's take could be just as legitimate as yours transforms conflict into an opportunity for connection and growth.

Ponder What You Don't Know

Did you notice how often Robin and Pat dove under the surface of the conflict that they were in to build meanings, assess values, and evaluate relationships upon a set of flawed assumptions? A look to the ceiling confirms lack of interest; a clarification of terms on a form confirms disrespect. Once we're in conflict, we're very good at constructing meanings from the smallest things, meanings that pile on evidence to prove that we are right.

Imagine this scenario. Instead of jumping to certainty about meanings, values, and relationships, what if Robin and Pat embraced uncertainty and curiosity about those very things? We are convinced that there is a form of not knowing that is very powerful, a sort of benevolent ignorance that can shape one's attitude in conflict to great effect. Paradoxically, not knowing can be a form of knowing.

Let's walk through how that can work. To be sure, during conflict our brains make a powerful commitment to our own sticky perspective. As we saw in chapter 3, in conflict we can defend ourselves by stitching bits and pieces of behavior, speech, and context into an overarching story that's very convincing. In those moments, we can feel absolutely certain that we know, and that knowledge can feel powerful.

But it's an illusory, puny power. It gives you no additional information outside of your confirmation bias; it closes down instead of opening up your perspective. It's like a broken record, reiterating a limited understanding that is flawed from the start.

That's why accepting that you don't know can be a source of knowledge. If you recognize that your very convincing story is limited and limiting, it opens up other possibilities, vantage points, insights. Strangely enough, giving up the puny power of your certainty gives you access to a far greater power and far more useful knowledge.

Name Power, Bias, and Privilege

Over the years, we've had fascinating discussions with workshop participants over the role of the director in this conflict scenario. As an authority figure, the director looms large over Pat, who lacks a sense of trust and alignment with them. Given that Pat is doing this work to serve their home community, this lack of trust and alignment is disempowering. Instead of engaging with the conflict that is disrupting the very interactions their shared work requires, Pat steps back, feeling no sense of support when it's needed most.

What about Robin's relationship to the director? Robin seems oblivious to the privilege of having a trusting, comfortable relationship to this supervisor, and unaware that Pat does not have that sort of relationship. That awareness would not only shed light on Pat's quick interaction with the director—an interaction that Robin interprets without hesitating to mean that all is well on Pat's end. That awareness would also reveal that, unlike the director's relationship to Pat, the director provides Robin with a sense of security and confidence.

Read more about bias and anti-racism in the NAEYC Advancing Equity in Early Childhood Education Position Statement.

Of course, a lack of awareness about power and privilege does not mean they don't exist. For that reason, we urge you to think long and hard about the power inherent in that tangle of supervisory relationships. This exploration is particularly important if you are a supervisor. For those you supervise, your status is certainly a central component of their conflicts with you. Think of your own conflict experiences with your supervisors: weren't you keenly aware of those dynamics?

To provide you with lots of opportunities to see where your assumptions may lie, we have intentionally built several important features into the case studies. The names "Robin" and "Pat" are gender neutral. The cases focus on a set of specific episodes that the two characters share but experience quite differently due to their own perspectives—perspectives that could be shaped in many distinct ways by culture, language, demographics, and the like. So, while every single detail is very important, it's also true that there are a multitude of different reasons why those details are important.

Unpack Your Own Assumptions and Bias

Dig a bit into the case study that you found more compelling. What aspects of gender, age, race, language, sexuality, culture, education, experience, or ability were you assuming about Robin or Pat? Did you assume that the character was like you in those ways, or was the character different? What details did you select to support those assumptions?

Now try these thought experiments. What happens if you change that character's gender, education level, or race? Does your perspective on the situation change? Walk through Pat and Robin's stories again, changing another characteristic such as language, age, or ability. Does your perspective of their experiences shift?

It's likely that your first interpretation included assumptions that align with your identity. If you found yourself agreeing with Robin that Pat was at fault, your assumptions are actually forms of bias. Those biases are not only singular, connected to our individual perspectives, but also collective, connected to structural privileges and inequities that impact all of our workplaces. We believe that these biases are extremely important for each person to unpack and explore, for they go to the heart of so many of the conflicts that we see.

For example, we have learned in our work that institutionalized racism is very often at the heart of workplace conflict, with white cultural norms providing the foundation for institutional values, behavioral expectations, and communication styles. What if Robin and the director are middle-aged White men with bachelor's degrees, and Pat is a younger Latina who has yet to finish her associate's degree? Does that change your perspective on the situation?

We urge you to explore these issues, not only in relationship to the assumptions you couldn't help but make about Robin, Pat, and the others in the story but also by considering other possibilities. Where did your biases reveal themselves? Read more about bias and anti-racism in the NAEYC Advancing Equity in Early Childhood Education Position Statement at naeyc.org/resources/position-statements/equity.

Remember That Identity Is Sticky—Even When It's Not "Yours"

Did you find that you were contributing additional support to Robin's critique of Pat when reading that first story? And were you somewhat resistant at the outset of Pat's tale to let yourself see things from this new perspective? Finally, were you able to find parts of your own identity in one or both stories?

In our workshops, we are continually amazed that participants get so invested in the role play. As their voices rise and their laughter starts to cascade, we walk around to hear what people are saying—and it's very interesting stuff. "I can't believe you did that to me." "Who do you think you are?" "Oh, come on, that's not what you were doing." Referring to themselves and their partners as if they are the people that they are role-playing, workshop participants declare things that make them sound, to us, like people in the midst of real conflicts.

Look and Listen for Erased and Silenced People

We close this chapter on a sobering note. Workshop after workshop, year after year, at the end of the raucous discussions about Robin and Pat, we ask our audiences the following:

"Please raise your hand if, during your role-play conversation, you discussed the parent or child in the last episode of each scenario."

As we now have come to expect—but to the great shock of the participants in the audience—despite attendance in the hundreds, we have never seen more than three or four hands in the air at a time.

Folks who work in early childhood education do not do it for social prestige. We do not do it for hefty salaries. Our generally inadequate recognition as a field in terms of both recognition and pay are well documented. No, like Robin and Pat, we folks work in our profession to serve the children and families in our care. This is why finding your way through conflict is such an important part of that work. If you do not learn these skills, *conflict will erase and silence the very people you seek to serve.*

To be sure, putting these skills into action is harder to do in real life and in the moment than in a workshop. We rarely have the luxury of time and distance away from such conflicts, and we certainly don't get opportunities to exchange written case studies describing our perspective. But, as we said at the start of the chapter, the experience of feeling embedded in these roles helps emphasize the important lessons from earlier chapters.

The mess that Robin and Pat created left us with a trail of breadcrumbs that help point to a better way through conflict. Developing a sense of what you bring into a conflict, collaborating with the little stuff to build trust, and taking the time to develop an understanding of another's perspective: all of these elements were missing from Robin and Pat's situation and are crucial to the conflict engagement strategies we lay out in the next three chapters.

CHAPTER 5

STARTING WITH YOURSELF

Let's take a quick look back to review the perspectives, attitudes, and insights we've covered. This will help you to engage in preliminary steps toward slow, deliberate responsiveness. After that review, we use the rest of the chapter to assign you some self-reflective tasks that are opportunities for you to take that backward step to engage your observing self.

After all, the only self in this conflict that you have any hope to manage with skill is your own self—a lifelong project if ever there was one.

Helpful Reminders as You Prepare to Prepare

Slow and steady is, truly, the only way forward. Take your time to read through these sections, pausing to reflect anywhere that feels tricky or sticky. We've added a question or two to the end of each section to help with that reflection; feel free to grab a pen or call a friend to write or talk them through. When you are feeling fairly steady underfoot, move to the next section.

Don't Forget That Conflicts Are Opportunities

Remember the quotation from Stone, Patton, and Heen that we shared in the introduction? Here it is again: "Dealing constructively with tough topics and awkward situations strengthens a relationship. And that's an opportunity too good to pass up."

Conflicts reveal things that are often hard for us and others to see, and those things expose the frayed edges or weak fabric of the relationships we find ourselves in. That exposure can be dispiriting or empowering, depending on how you approach the tough topics and awkward situations the conflict engenders.

That's the rub, isn't it? Like so many situations in life, in order for a conflict to be an opportunity, you have to believe that it is an opportunity. Entering a conflict holding tight to your confirmation bias is a guarantee that you'll gain nothing but smug, misguided satisfaction—and you'll perpetuate the problem that has been nagging you all the while. Given that outcome, why bother engaging at all? On the other hand, if you decide that, thanks to the tough topics and awkward situations, you have a genuine opportunity to strengthen your relationship, it'd be unfortunate not to try.

Think of the benefits. Right now, you're likely tip-toeing around the person, unsure of even the most minute interactions, or angrily avoiding them at the expense of your composure at work. The fact that you're not taking this conflict as an opportunity is actually creating an inhospitable workplace for you.

> By approaching your conflict with your counterpart as an opportunity to improve that relationship, you can have a direct, positive impact on the very people you are serving.

Consider that carefully. If you're stuck in blame, it can feel counterintuitive to believe that you are creating this problem, or at least that you are avoiding solving it. But it's a simple fact: in most of these situations, you are the person who is experiencing this conflict as a disruption to your work. Whatever your counterpart is feeling—and it may be very little—your experience is likely pretty lousy.

As we've learned, that disruption seeps out into everything you do. When you're dysregulated, you create dysregulation around you; without you realizing it, your whole workplace may be permeated by your reaction to this conflict.

What's more, we know that a toxic relationship or workplace environment is damaging to children and families. So think of it this way: by approaching your conflict with your counterpart as an opportunity to improve that relationship, you can have a direct, positive impact on the very people you are serving.

Consider two or three examples of conflicts you have experienced that felt like opportunities and two or three examples that did not. How are these similar and how are they different?

Now, focus on the situations that did not feel like opportunities. How can the similarities you identified help shift your thinking? Consider also the potential to have a direct, positive impact on families and children.

Recognize That Patience Is a Virtue (and a Practical Investment)

So often in conflict, every fiber of our being urges us to dive in. That's why we have woven patience into every page of this book. Finding your way through conflict requires hefty doses of it.

Our neurology and neurochemistry drive us to react; taking the time to pause, breathe, and reflect activates bodily systems that support responsive engagement. Our initially held assumptions, attitudes, and perspectives are dangerously limited; taking the time to ask questions about those limitations helps to dissolve assumptions, soften attitudes, and broaden perspectives. Because our stories about what happened seem firm and fixed, taking the time to ask about and listen to another's story is the only chance we have to sort things out.

Like most virtues, however, patience doesn't feel very virtuous when you really need to use it. Instead, it can feel like stalling—and not just to you. So we want to make an additional case for patience, one that is less moral and more practical. Patience is an excellent investment. Over and over again, we have watched eager people dive into conflicts with brazen confidence, a few tools, and far too little time invested, only to make matters worse. Their very enthusiasm, untempered by patience, becomes the impediment to finding their way through conflict.

We see this in our schools all the time when it comes to conflicts with parents. A teacher comes to our office, flummoxed by an angry arrival or accusatory departure. Very often, it's not the teacher's fault; instead, someone else in the room did or didn't do something, and they're left to sort out what happened. Meanwhile, no one is actually interested in figuring out what the parent is thinking or feeling. They are just a problem to be solved—and when a human is a problem to solve, things are going from bad to worse.

We've learned that this is the moment to embrace patience not as a moral principle but as a practical benefit. That three- or four-minute exchange between parent and teacher was too little time to sort out the problem, much less address it productively. But lurking in that problem is an important insight into conflict, one that reveals an excellent investment opportunity.

Teachers typically perceive such moments with families as revealing a lack of trust. To them, it's clear that the parent does not trust them, their colleagues, and their program. We think that's almost always exactly wrong.

When you take a bit of time to step into the conflict, you learn that the story is more complicated. Most of the time, we find that parents are investing trust in us precisely by bringing up a difficult topic with rough feelings around it. After all, they are doing something that involves genuine risk to the child in your care, a child that they entrust to you many hours each day. Over and over, we learn that activating that trust with patient, explicit gratitude is the right move.

It's surprisingly easy to do. We have learned that, when we say to a parent, "Thank you for bringing that up. I'm sure it was very hard to do," the scenario tends to flip. Suddenly, the angry parent appreciates that you want a positive relationship with them and their family; you've softened their anger by affirming the trust they so desperately want to maintain.

We typically find our hunch affirmed when we say, "I'm not sure what happened here, but if you can give me a day to sort it all out, I'll make sure at least one of us sits down with you to figure out how to regain your trust." Suddenly, what seemed an urgent demand is now placed within the broader context of an ongoing relationship, one that needs time and attention. All it took was injecting a little bit of calm patience.

Instead of a hurried three-minute exchange, patient, relatively brief conversation saves you dozens of urgent, reactive hours. Patience truly is more than a virtue. It's sound economics!

When are you most patient, and least patient, in conflict?

What do those situations have in common?

Consider the example above about the angry parent. What could you say in your conflict situations to activate patience and build or rebuild trust?

Remember the Core Principles About Conflict

Back in the introduction, we laid out a set of six core principles that we asked you to keep in mind throughout the book. They've been appearing in different forms in the previous chapters, but we think they are good reminders as we move into negotiating the conflict itself.

Conflict Is Natural, Normal, and Deeply Human

By now, we hope that you've accepted a happy fact: your relationship to conflict is not proof that you are a terrible, no-good, very bad person. It's just proof that you're a person. You're on the human path through conflict, stumbling along with the rest of us.

The path is, frankly, a noble one. It means that you're encountering people, situations, and a world that doesn't comply with your preconceived notions and deeply held desires about what should and should not be. It means that you're confronting human existence as it swirls and changes—what we might call "reality."

Conflict Is the Work, Not a Distraction from the Work

Our work in early childhood (and, we would argue, nearly all work on the planet) is at its core collaborative. Those collaborations form the environment in which we create learning experiences for young children, humans who need secure attachments and trustworthy caregivers to scaffold those experiences. If a program has done its work, the caregivers are diverse, not latched to a particular culture, language, worldview, or perspective.

> Your relationship to conflict is not proof that you are a terrible, no-good, very bad person. It's just proof that you're a person. You're on the human path through conflict, stumbling along with the rest of us.

Because conflict is human, those collaborative, diverse experiences will routinely provoke conflict. Because humans never determine how to solve conflict once and for all, we need to learn from each conflict as it arises. Finally, because young children shut down around adults who are avoiding conflict, we need to model conflict engagement and response for them.

So, in early childhood settings, conflict is not a distraction from the work. It is not getting in the way of the work. It is not disconnected from the work. If you're reading this book on your own, this section—and indeed this whole chapter—might be the resource you need to engage your supervisor and colleagues in finding your way through conflict together.

Conflict is the work, and everyone—children and adults, employees and supervisors—needs to treat it as such.

Conflict Is Almost Always Reciprocal

Every once in a while, we learn about an interpersonal conflict that really, truly does seem one-sided. A toxic employee who treats everyone else with contempt. A parent confrontation that most teachers solve with composure but that one administrator believes is a conspiracy to undermine them. A family support employee who consistently refuses to work with certain people in the community.

These conflicts are less about interpersonal conflict and more about personnel dilemmas, best handled by your human resources department or immediate supervisor. They certainly exist, but we think that they are rare.

The vast majority of conflicts we've encountered in our work are reciprocal. When we hear someone critically railing against a coworker, we routinely point this out and ask if there are any ways that the critic has contributed to the conflict. They often hurriedly say, "Well, yes, I guess I did, but . . ."—and that's where we make them pause and ponder. There's a lot to learn in the "yes, I guess I did" before you get to the "but"!

Finally, we've also learned that there's still a lot to understand and learn even if a specific conflict is absolutely not at all your fault. How are you reacting to this one-sided affair? What assumptions and perspectives do you bring to it? Why are you caught up in response to this conflict that, you declare, has nothing to do with you? Seems to us that it's worth spending some time there.

Conflict Exists If Someone Says It Does

The flip side of the previous section, the idea that conflict exists if someone says it does, can be thought of as the "Who? Me? No!" principle. Every once in a while, you create a big mess without knowing it. When you do learn about it, you're suddenly confronted with both the mess itself and responsibility for having created it.

That's why we say that conflict exists if someone says it does. If nothing else, there is a deep conflict in terms of the way that you and others are perceiving the situation. It's time to accept the reality that your perception is limited, and those limitations have an impact on this situation. Neuroscience and psychology tell us that this happens all the time. Surely it can happen to you, right?

As you engage this principle, remember the distinction between blame and contribution. Just because you acknowledge that you've contributed in some way to a conflict doesn't mean capitulating to self-judgmental blame. As the previous principle suggests, it's rarely that simple.

Conflict Is Sustained by Win/Lose, Right/Wrong Thinking

Conflicts aren't competitions. Unfortunately, your neurochemistry, defensiveness, and much more will all be working hard to convince you otherwise. We aren't lawyers or debate coaches; we actually don't want you to defeat your opponent. We want you to find your way through conflict, because we're convinced that doing so can lead to a better workplace, stronger relationships, a more secure sense of your flawed, human self, and a more caring, compassionate world.

> **We want you to find your way through conflict, because we're convinced that doing so can lead to a better workplace, stronger relationships, a more secure sense of your flawed, human self, and a more caring, compassionate world.**

That means you have to drop out of the fictional lawsuit or tournament your reactivity fabricates. You need to let go of win/lose, right/wrong thinking. That said, we realize that right/wrong thinking is just about the stickiest thing there is in conflict. It's also an enormously powerful component of our win/lose culture, gaining more converts every day.

So if you are someone who is having a hard time giving it up, try this nimble twist, taken from Peter Elbow's book *Writing without Teachers*, and apply right/wrong thinking to yourself:

> You are always right and always wrong. . . .
>
> You are always right in that no one is ever in a position to tell you what you perceive and experience. You must have a kind of faith or trust: not that your perception is always accurate, but that the greatest accuracy comes from using it more and listening to it better. . . .
>
> But you are always wrong in that you never see accurately enough, experience fully enough. . . . You must always put more energy into trying to have other people's perceptions and experiences—trying to make yourself more agile, more flexible, more refined. Don't stubbornly stay locked into your own impressions just because they are yours (Elbow 1998, 106).

Conflict Never Stops Teaching Us

There's so much to learn from conflict, the complicated gift that—annoyingly, exhaustingly—keeps on giving and giving and giving. Since you'll never stop bumping into conflict, why not decide you'll try to learn from the darned thing?

> *Which principle seems most obvious to you?*
>
> *Which seems harder to hold as you lean into conflict—and why?*

Quick Overview of the Six Core Principles of Working Through Conflict

Learning how to work through conflict starts with understanding six core principles. The full description of these principles is on pages 78-80.

Conflict Is Natural, Normal, and Deeply Human

This principle, in a calm moment of reading, may appear completely obvious: conflict is a natural part of life, a normal component of social interaction that activates our deepest humanity. Of course, we don't feel that way when we are in conflict. Instead, we feel misunderstood. Everything is off kilter; our usual selves and skills have vanished, replaced by a clunky, demanding set of thoughts and feelings that do not reflect who we really are. But those feelings are precisely what connect us to the rest of humanity.

Conflict Is the Work, Not a Distraction from the Work

Nearly everyone who has attended our workshops over the years describes conflict as the thing that prevents them from doing their real work. We believe conflict is the work. But, as far as we are aware, few if any higher education programs, early childhood agencies, and professional development systems teach adult conflict as a core component of that work. So, instead of seeing conflict as an impediment or distraction, we place it front and center as the work itself—and, we're convinced, usually the most important work.

Conflict Is Almost Always Reciprocal

Conflicts typically drive us into a defensive posture. That's how the blame game begins: as we experience the problems created in the conflict, we extend our index finger to point out that their source exists elsewhere. Unfortunately for our egos, it's rarely that simple! In our experience, the majority of conflicts are reciprocal, which means that we've everyone contributed their fair share—even though they're usually well-meaning individuals trying to do what's right in tricky situations. To help you see your part of conflict, there are sections of the book where we prompt you to fess up to your role in the mess. And it turns out this is a very effective conflict resolution strategy all by itself!

Conflict Exists If Someone Says It Does

Routinely, the conflicts that have been brought to our attention seem one-sided, at least to one of the parties. In those situations, while the aggrieved person is feeling troubled, offended, disrespected, or worse, the other person doesn't even see the problem. We assert that, if one person declares a given situation is a conflict, then there's a conflict! The collaborative relationships between adults that drive most early childhood workplaces simply cannot function properly if one person is ignoring another person's concerns. So, if someone calls foul, it's time for both parties to make a good-faith effort to work it out.

Conflict Is Sustained by Win/Lose, Right/Wrong Thinking

Skillfully negotiating conflict is never just yes or no, easy or hard. In fact, conflict feeds off of that sort of either/or thinking; it's the gasoline that makes the engine run—and often splashes out of the tank, where a spark can set the car on fire! So to learn how best to negotiate conflict, you'll need to learn how to live in the middle—in the ambiguous zone—and that is a real challenge for most of us. Our families, our cultures, our educations, even our neurology: they all drive us into this sort of either/or thinking, so we teach you in the book how to resist it by developing a thorough understanding of how to avoid either/or perspectives as often as possible.

Define What You (and Consider What Other People) Mean by *Conflict*

In chapter 1, we explored some scenarios to help you examine your definition of conflict and explore how that definition differs from person to person. To find your way through conflict with greater ease and skill, it's crucial to hold on to both of those things at once: you want to know both what you identify as a conflict as well as what other people might consider a conflict—a perspective that, in conflict, you might otherwise overlook.

> **Each person in a conflict brings a set of meanings, values, and relationships based on their unique life experiences. These form the underlying foundation of how we react in any situation, and especially in conflicts.**

That's sometimes a challenge, but we have faith in you. After all, a significant portion of being an early childhood educator is anticipating and reading real-time social cues that humans reveal through their behavior and words. You know how to recognize when a baby is tired, when a conflict is brewing between preschoolers, and when a family might need support as they approach a transition. This same kind of attentiveness to your own reactions as well as the reactions of others will help you quickly mitigate tricky situations.

Frequently, as school directors, the two of us check in with teachers when something seems "off" with them: a slightly quickened pace as they walk through our office door, avoiding eye contact when they usually pause and smile, and the like. Often teachers are surprised that we noticed, saying, "How did you know I was upset?"

To be sure, it is often difficult to invite yourself into someone else's tension and offer to help explore it. So we need to be able to explain that we aren't *seeking* conflict when we do so. Rather, we are trying to clarify how someone is experiencing conflict, and we do that by initiating recognition and connection. If we do it with a light touch, noting that someone is "off" and asking to understand can build trust in ways that nothing else can.

What is your definition of conflict?

How is this the same or different from how your colleagues would define conflict?

Ponder the Organizational and Cultural Contexts

Despite how intelligent, perceptive, or open-minded you are, there is always more happening in a situation than you perceive at first. Have you noticed that, even when a conflict seems small and easily solvable, you discover more and more when you start exploring? Yes, we're back to finding icebergs, and we need to find those meanings, values, and relationships below the surface.

Each person in a conflict brings a set of meanings, values, and relationships based on their unique life experiences. These form the underlying foundation of how we react in any situation, and especially in conflicts. Meanwhile, in the workplace, our experiences are situated within a specific organizational culture with its own set of meanings, values, and relationships. We need to understand how those two sets interact at work, not only above the surface where we define things specifically but also below the surface.

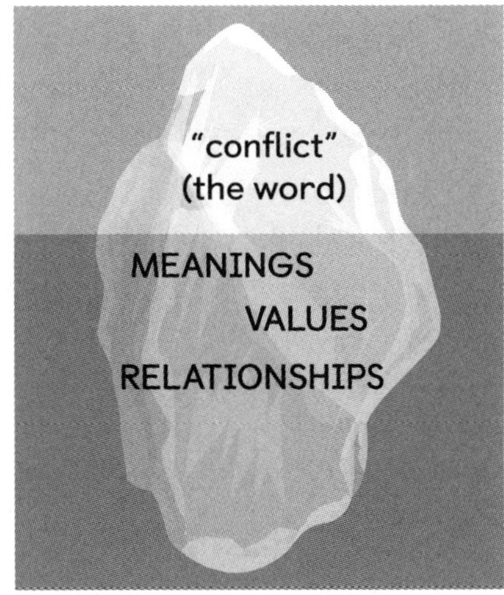

In a conflict, it's beneficial to ask yourself about one more iceberg: your counterpart has their own set of meanings, values, and relationships in play here. You probably don't agree with all of them, and you may not like some of them very much. But you'll find your way through conflict with greater skill and ease if you ponder that iceberg carefully too.

Draw an iceberg. What exists above and below the surface for you?

Draw a second iceberg. Identify what exists above the surface for the people you work with.

Leave the space of the iceberg below the surface blank as a reminder to make space for what you don't know or understand about others.

Analyze Sticky Details as Autobiography

Throughout the book, we've been using a lot of stories about ourselves, our colleagues, and several fictional characters. Those stories are intentionally populated with lots and lots of details: bumper stickers, missing artwork, and one very bad interaction with a parent filling out a form. Some seem meaningless at first; several are quite embarrassing to us.

We added all of those details because we have found that they are like the little curls at the end of Velcro strands, subtle little hooks that make otherwise unimportant things stick like crazy. Paying close attention to what sticks is the key to understanding who you are in conflict.

Details matter. They slow you down in a good way, preventing you from moving to broad, general accusations and forcing you to be patient. They disrupt assumptions you've made about a person or a situation, adding nuance. They suggest other ways into someone's story.

And they are autobiographical: a telling detail says more about you than about anyone else. If you're brave enough, the details that stick out to you are little keys to the closet you like to keep locked. Exploring why a given detail nags at you is a way into understanding what you value, what threatens you, what any given conflict engages.

So use details to help you understand yourself. (Soon enough, you'll extend the same approach to your counterpart.)

What sorts of details are stickiest for you in conflict?

Flip from Intent to Impact and Back Again. Repeat.

You carry intent into conflict every time. A situation that has suddenly gone sideways can catch you by surprise, and intent is the reason. A stray comment, a forgotten task, a facial expression you didn't know you made can all set you back on your heels when someone raises a conflict.

You know you are operating in the world of intent when that all-too-familiar phrase pops into your head: "But I didn't mean to!" What you meant to do is always important. However, it's not the only thing that's important.

We urge you to take advantage of the moments when that phrase forms in your brain. It's a sure sign that you're feeling defensive and that your defensiveness is backing you into a corner. Instead, flip it around, and recognize that your intent is not the whole story. Start asking and thinking about impact, about what happened to other people when you did the thing that was meaningful to you.

There's a silver lining here that folks often overlook. When you flip to impact, you don't erase intent. Admitting to someone that your impact may differ from your intent affords them the ability to see the difference as well. Suddenly, two people are expanding their notion of what happened and why, dislodging the sorts of limited logic that clog an effective response.

That is to say, flipping between impact and intent allows both parties to engage other perspectives while maintaining their own—a critical strategy to have on hand. Indeed, we have repeatedly found that this simple distinction can have a profound effect on even the stickiest conflicts, for others and for ourselves. So keep flipping. It'll do you lasting good!

When can you get stuck on intent?

When is it hardest to see the impact of your actions?

Acknowledge Rupture and Commit to Repair

This insight follows from the last. All human relationships have ups and downs, and since you're imperfect like the rest of us, you're going to find yourself doing something that has a negative impact on another person. It's inevitable.

Acknowledging the impactful rupture that your actions create is a very powerful act. It signals to another person that you want to be in the reality of your relationship, instead of sitting in some happy fiction where nothing ever goes wrong. It also opens the door for them to explore their own role in the rupture—which is almost surely part of the situation.

Acknowledging rupture is itself an act of repair. Sometimes we encounter folks who are so distraught about a problem that confronting it is very difficult—and doing so with another person nearly unthinkable. But that's the mysterious power of acknowledgment. Simply admitting that a problem exists is, all by itself, a way to move out of the problem and explore other possibilities.

> **Acknowledging rupture is itself an act of repair.**

You don't need instant solutions, quick fixes, and the like. Your acknowledgment is itself the best first step, a statement that commits you to repair. Indeed, usually it's the only first step that's available.

Which of your actions are most likely to cause ruptures that are difficult to repair?

Engage the Four Attitudes

When we talk with folks at our workshops, we often find ourselves discussing their conflicts in a manner that they report is unusual. Both of us do our best to listen intently and engage the participant's perspective with respect. But then something shifts.

Somewhere in the midst of that conversation, we might toss in a self-deprecating comment about how we've fumbled around with the same problem ourselves and have no off-the-shelf solution. Or Christine will turn to Chris and say, "That's what you were doing to me last week." Or Chris might ask Christine, "You were struggling with that at your school. What happened there?"

These moments reveal the extent to which we reject the idea that we are know-it-all experts in conflict studies. Instead, we perform the four attitudes of *nonjudgmental reflection, humble curiosity, self-effacing humor,* and *accepting imperfection.* By doing so, we walk the participant into a radically different relationship to the very problem that brought them to the workshop in the first place.

It takes some effort and practice to learn how to adopt these sorts of attitudes. That said, most of the early childhood educators that we know are thoughtful, dedicated people who chose the field based on their values and principles. You may already have your own concepts, taken from your spiritual, community, or cultural lives, that align with these attitudes, concepts like *grace* and *inquiry.* Even if you have such concepts handy, why not adopt these four?

Which of the four attitudes is easiest or most natural for you?

Which feel awkward, fake, or scary?

Recognize Your Brain States

Brains are complex organs, and while we would like to think that we are always capable of thinking rationally with our emotions under tight control, we know that's not always the case. Hormones produced by stress can cause our thinking skills to take a back burner to our brain's need to ensure safety and emotional security.

Our brains shift between learning, emotional, and security states, often without our keen awareness of that shift. So it's both necessary and beneficial for us to pay attention to our brain state when we're in it (as best we can) and then reflect on the impact it has had on our ability to engage in conflict productively and reflectively.

Admittedly, recognizing your brain state is a demanding cognitive action, one that your brain will push back against in order to put all energy into the survival and emotional states. Creating a habit of paying attention to your brain state will allow you to quickly identify what you need, work through the brain state, and get to the thinking part of the process.

The Survival State: Am I Safe?

Fight, flight, or freeze: this trio describes your brain's quick checklist to measure your response to hazard and risk. We often think of this process in relation to an obvious physical threat: a bear near our campsite, a tornado off in the distance. But life isn't as straightforward as a Warner Bros. cartoon, and we don't need a falling anvil to make us fight, flight, or freeze. Even without the presence of an obvious physical threat, stress hormones can still take over our bodies and brains.

Of course, you don't have to remain in a conflict that presents a true threat; you may need to change the setting or the people involved to feel safe. If you are confronted in a small, isolated area by an untrusted, untested colleague, a fear reaction could be reasonable. It's helpful to have the ability to measure the threat and take quick action to move to a public space, ask for a mediator, or request another time to discuss your differences.

More often, we find that you may just need to be aware of the physical changes in your body that are occurring and remind yourself of how you know you are safe. You are in a trusted work environment. You have support systems in place for handling difficult situations. You and the person you are in conflict with have the same good intention: to act on the best interests of children. (If those things are not true, it's time to talk to your supervisor about your workplace conditions.)

Sadly, we don't have control over the occurrence of our physiological stress responses. But we can engage in careful reflection and action to work through this troubling brain state.

What happens in your body when you feel unsafe?

How can you know that you're safe in a conflict situation?

What steps can you take to help your body return to a calmer state?

The Emotional State: Am I Loved?

In many ways, the establishing of physical safety is fairly simple to describe: choose a space you find comfortable, ensure that you have trusted people to help mediate, and so on. But we all know that even once we are physically safe, the situation can still feel emotionally risky.

The truth is that risk is built into the human enterprise. After all, there's only one way to establish emotional security with another person, and that's through connection. In the case of conflict, emotional security requires connection to the person you are in conflict with—a risky enterprise if ever there was one! But remember this: just as you need a connection with them to move on from the emotional state, they need that connection with you too.

> **Without some sort of emotional connection, you're going to remain stuck in this conflict. So be brave and take the risk of connection.**

Tricky, right? This connection with another person doesn't mean you're going to be best friends; there's no perfect relationship at the end of the conflict rainbow. But without some sort of emotional connection, you're going to remain stuck in this conflict. So be brave and take the risk of connection, with some understanding of what skin you have in the game.

What happens in your body when you're in the emotional state of asking "Am I loved?"

What feelings are easier for you to name?

What prohibits you from acknowledging the feelings of another person?

The Executive State: What Can I Learn?

Physically safe? Check. Emotionally safe? Check. You can now return to the comfortable space of thinking and communicating logically. You can begin to work through the details of the situation and work toward a solution. Right?

Not quite. The catch here is that both people need to be truly ready to move on, not just you. Because of the vulnerability you experience when you have strong emotions, you might be eager to get out of that state and hurry over the step of establishing that necessary connection for both people. We see this all the time: "Yay! I'm ready to fix, to solve, to go go GO!" And suddenly everything is back at square one.

How do you know if you're ready to move on from the emotional brain state to the executive brain state?

How do you know if the other person is ready to move on?

Distinguish Behavior from Identity

We smile when we hear phrases like "I finally got to see her true self!" and "I *knew* that's what was going on!" Those confident declarations are indications that someone's confirmation bias is hard at work on a very specific, and very dangerous, project: equating behavior and identity.

> **Factors related to power, bias, and privilege are always part of social interactions and thus of conflict.**

As early childhood educators, we know the risks of this equation. Saying that a preschool child who struggles with transitions is "temperamental" or that a toddler who says "No!" when you ask her to do something is "defiant": these are violations of our understanding of basic child development. We know we must treat behaviors as developmental indicators, not as proof that a child "is" something or someone: "bad," "troubled," or worse.

Of course, that is exactly what your brain does in conflict with your counterpart. So *you* need to separate annoying, troubling, or otherwise frustrating behavior from the person who did it—especially when you are in conflict with them. You'll never find your way through conflict without that distinction.

> *What behaviors—what this person did—are confirming your sense of identity and your assumptions about who this person is?*

> *What other behaviors, past or present, would disrupt your confirmation bias about who this person is?*

> *Where might you find some grace for this human being?*

Sniff Out Power, Bias, and Privilege

There's no way around it: factors related to power, bias, and privilege are always part of social interactions and thus of conflict. Those factors can be subtle, particularly for those who are in the privileged position in a given power dynamic, but they are no less impactful due to their subtlety (or your ignorance of them).

It's tempting to start looking for these factors in your opponent's behavior, of course. But our task here is to start from humility and consider your own position within those power dynamics. A careful consideration of how such factors are at play for you can broaden your ability to think open-mindedly and implement practices that make more space for differences.

Power dynamics exist in a number of demographic areas, such as racial and gender dynamics, ableism and ethnocentrism, and more. In addition, power dynamics in education settings can be connected to the position a person holds, an employee's tenure, existing or perceived relationships with people in positions of power, and so on. Understanding the power you have can help ensure you don't unintentionally use it manipulatively or unfairly. Finally, there's a good chance that your counterpart is very much aware of that power in this conflict—it may be constraining their or your ability to address the conflict at all.

> *What actual or perceived power do you have that your counterpart does not?*

> *What biases do you have that may be impacting your ability to hear and understand your colleague's perspective?*

Activate the Observing, Professional Self

Our last review item might as well be the subtitle to our book! Taking the backwards step to allow your observing, professional self to reflect is essential, the patient pause along the side of the road to explore exactly where you've been, where you are, and how you'll get to where you want to go. You just can't find your way through conflict without it.

We've chosen the three words *observing, professional self* that we think are very important for this suggestion. You can't keep your fingers crossed that your observing self will appear when you most need it; you can't rely on your professional self saving the day when you're flailing around in a conflict. No, you must activate your observing, professional self; you need to make a conscious decision to turn it on when the need arises.

The rest of the chapter provides four tasks to do just that.

What sorts of conflict allow you to take a step backwards and observe yourself?

When is that observing, professional self most difficult to activate?

The Four Personal Preparation Tasks

If you've been able to answer the reflection questions above with ease, confidence, and honesty, then the four tasks ahead will be straightforward. If, however, the tasks seem daunting or perplexing, scan the questions above for hints about where you're getting stuck. A current, detailed conflict will help you engage these sections more powerfully. Perhaps you have one in mind already. If not, think of a sticky one from the recent past that will allow you to self-reflect.

Personal Task 1: Check Your Purposes

We are routinely surprised by workshop participants who seem befuddled when we ask them a simple question: "Why do you want to address this conflict?" To us, it's a pretty straightforward question. After all, they are taking a good chunk of time to attend a workshop to help them with it.

Sometimes, we suspect, the question is befuddling because the person has never asked it of themselves. When they do, it's not exactly clear what they should make of it. There's an urgency to solving the conflict, to be sure, but they can't put their finger on where that urgency comes from.

When you have moments like these—and we all do!—there's a good chance that you're not in an optimal brain state to answer questions. When words fail but situations feel urgent, that's a sign that your executive state isn't engaged, and that the parts of your brain that help you find words aren't active. Time to take that step backward, breathe deeply a few times, and ask the question again.

Ready to reflect and learn? Then let's try again. Why, exactly, do you want to address this conflict? What do you hope to accomplish? What outcomes do you seek?

Activate that observing self and take a look at this list of possible answers:

- It's time for someone to stand up to this jerk.

- You're done with them and they need to know it.

- They always get what they want—but not this time!

- You're right, and they need to understand that they are wrong.

- This nonsense has to stop once and for all!

Winning, being right, triumph, justification . . . we can just imagine the crowd cheering our victory! In conflict we have all been there; most of the time, this is where we start. Our brains and bodies are designed to feed lots of energy into this sort of thinking, but it's the starting point, and not the end point, to figuring out your purposes in conflict.

Sometimes the observing self observes some ugly stuff, doesn't it? Time to activate the observing, *professional* self now.

Take a look at this list of possible descriptors for what is happening with a counterpart at work:

- Your relationship to this person isn't working the way you want, and you want to change that.

- This person is pushing your buttons for some reason, and you're hoping that working together you can sort that out.

- You have moments of feeling that this person doesn't really respect you, but that just doesn't make sense. You need to understand why that's happening.

- You're pretty sure that both of you can figure out ways to collaborate more effectively if you try.

- Something complicated is going on, and you need to figure out what it is.

- You are getting in each other's hair a lot, and you need a few small moments of shared success.

The person processing these considerations sounds like someone who wants to do a better job at work, who thinks that things are not quite right and can be fixed with a bit of attention and care, who knows that they are human and that others are human too. In short, it sounds like a professional.

You are much more likely to find your way through conflict if you know what you want to accomplish by engaging it. We encourage you to consider goals that have the following qualities.

They are learning goals. You've got your humble curiosity out front and center. You know that there's something happening here, but you don't know what it is, and you're going to find out.

They are collaborative. You know you can't do this alone, whatever "this" turns out to be. You've been chewing on this alone for a while, and you keep running into questions that only your counterpart can answer.

They are long-term. Sure, you want to fix a specific problem or situation, but you realize that your short-term desires are band-aids covering a bigger issue. That means that you are taking a first step, not reaching the end of the path.

They are grounded in relationship. When it's all said and done, what you want is a mostly respectful, mostly thoughtful relationship with a work colleague. Of course, sometimes they'll drive you nuts—and you'll do the same. But you want those moments to be exceptions, not the norm. You want a healthier relationship, and therefore a healthier workplace.

> Our decision to engage in a tense discussion might be in defense of who we are or what we stand for.

To sort out your purposes, take a moment to reflect on this scenario: It's six months later. You have an encounter with your counterpart, but everything has changed.

What happens?

What do you do? What do they do?

What does it feel like to you? To them? To your colleagues? To the children and families you serve?

Now look through the qualities above and consider them through the lens of your scenario. Write down a few thoughts about what you want to accomplish.

Personal Task 2: Ground Your Identity

Identity in conflict is a big deal. While it may linger under the surface, it is a large contributor to how we show up and perform in conflicts. In fact, it may have everything to do with why we even engage in a conflict at all. Our decision to engage in a tense discussion might be in defense of who we are or what we stand for.

Imagine that you find out a colleague has been complaining to other people about your leaving work early on Fridays. Of course, you know the reason: you need to leave early to pick up your child from a standing appointment, and you have communicated that to the appropriate people. But the fact that others are talking about you behind your back challenges both your integrity and your sense of responsibility as a parent.

How would your identity be engaged in this conflict? Consider what you would risk losing if you did or didn't engage in it: the respect of your peers? Your identity as a dependable colleague? Your confidence as a supportive parent?

Now turn from this example and toward the conflict within which you find yourself. What aspects of your identity are vulnerable? In what ways have you experienced respect or disrespect? Where is the line between reasonable risk and productive discomfort on the one hand, and dangerous hazards and pain on the other?

Here are some steps you can take to ground your identity:

Name and own the factors connected to your identity. What is relevant in this conflict situation that relates to your character or how you see yourself? How is your identity showing up in this conflict? Be aware of those factors as you take the next steps—they are important and powerful.

Take care of yourself. Gather affirmations that empower you. Reflect on your core values and beliefs. Name your strengths and positive contributions to the work. Remember the brain states and give yourself some time to breathe and work through the survival and emotional states.

Lean on your people. Find your squad and get their help as you prepare for engaging with your counterpart. And remember: unpacking a conflict situation with someone you trust and who knows you well is not gossip. Rather, it is a valuable strategy that can help you explore how your identity is coming into play in that relationship. Be sure to pick someone who is removed from the situation to avoid adding to workplace tension and creating unproductive additional problems.

Make a list: Who are your people that you can lean on that know you well and can provide an impartial ear?

Make a second list: What do you need to do to feel affirmed in a situation that feels challenging?

Personal Task 3: Understand Your Emotional Stake

Look through all the places in this book where you got pissed off, frustrated, or annoyed at us, your counterpart, or yourself. Know where your buttons are.

Once you know those locations, figure out what boundaries you want to put up to protect them. You are not signing up for abuse. You are not making yourself vulnerable to be attacked. So know what you need to protect and how you're going to protect it.

Make a list of acceptable frustrations and annoyances, challenges to your assumptions and biases that make sense, and then make a list of the things that you will not accept in the discussion.

Personal Task 4: Own Your Story and Prepare to Expand It

We have met a lot of wonderful, caring people in our decades in early childhood education. They truly seem like the sorts of caregivers we would want to work with us in our schools, dedicated to providing support to the children and families they serve.

Unfortunately, those same traits can be very risky in conflict.

When we first started our workshops, we didn't have this step. But as we worked through the other three steps with participants, helping them to secure their purpose, identity, and triggers, we noticed those traits of dedication and support coming to the fore.

To our surprise, many participants were taking those three steps as a prescription for disappearing into the conflict. It was as if the preparation confirmed what they had known all along: the only way to resolve the conflict was to make themselves and their story disappear. And that, of course, just meant that the conflict dug deeper and deeper into the relationship.

That's why we created this final step, which we have learned is very important for many folks. Conflicts can't be resolved by erasing one of the participants; conflicts can only be resolved when all parties come to understand the perspectives and stories of each other.

So we want you to own your story, not set it aside. We want you to take the time to clarify it, to identify the nuances that make it meaningful for you. That way, when you share it with another person, you are representing not only what happened but what matters to you. Identifying the meaning in the details is critical for any real resolution.

As you do that, remember that you are writing your story, a vital story to be sure. But it is limited, constrained by your perspective. So keep Peter Elbow's quotation in mind: you are always right, and you are always wrong.

As objectively as you can, write down your description of what happened from your perspective. Look through it for leaky spots—judgments, assumptions, generalizations. Commit both to its legitimacy and to its limitations.

We hope that you're now ready to reengage with your counterpart. To recap, here the four steps you just learned in preparation:

1. Check your purposes

2. Ground your identity

3. Understand your emotional stake

4. Own your story and prepare to expand it

You've got your squad and your story in place, and you have a sense of what you do and do not want to bring into the discussion.

But before you dive into that discussion, you need to do some preparation with your counterpart.

CHAPTER 6

BUILDING AND REBUILDING TRUST

Conflict shatters trust. Like so many aspects of this work, it sounds obvious, doesn't it? But, like other "obvious" points—*conflict is important to define* and *you are in your conflicts—conflict shatters trust* is a statement that deserves a lot more attention than it usually receives.

In our work relationships, we typically develop trust with colleagues as part of a shared commitment to children (and some trust that an employee was properly vetted in the hiring process). That trust can develop and grow over time, creating an authentic working relationship. Conflict shatters trust by challenging our sense of what is consistent and true in our relationships. Conflict raises doubts and it confirms suspicions.

When we feel connected to someone, whether personally or professionally, we harbor a host of unspoken inferences. We see ourselves and our values in the other person. We assume that our goals, perspectives, and attitudes are largely aligned. We pay attention to the same things; we identify and solve problems mutually. We reassure ourselves that, at fundamental levels, we are on the same page.

Conflict challenges our inferences, disconnecting us and disrupting our understanding of the relationship we thought we understood. Our sense of security is replaced with defensiveness and our confidence is undermined by skepticism and doubt. Disappointment mocks our earlier, suddenly naïve beliefs in people's goodness, integrity, and respect.

In this chapter, we focus entirely on that shattered trust. The strategies we lay out here in the second step to engage and resolve conflict both require trust and seek to rebuild it. You're also going to have to trust the process itself: it will take some faith and courage to make this all work.

But first, let's take a look at the components of trust itself.

Trust = Empathy + Logic + Authenticity

From the research of Harvard Business School professor Frances Frei, we know of a neat, powerful trio of components that, when added together, create trust. In her excellent TED

Talk, "How to Build (and Rebuild) Trust," Frei delineates the three components as *empathy*, *logic*, and *authenticity* (Frei 2018). Let's look at each one in turn.

The first component is immediately recognizable to most people. *Empathy* describes a person's ability to understand and share someone else's thoughts and feelings enacted through a caring connection. It's that sense that someone else can relate to what we're going through and is showing us that we matter. We communicate empathy by nodding, making eye contact, and other physical gestures. We perform our empathy by looping, which is the process of inquiring about, restating, and acknowledging what the other person is saying.

Those bodily and verbal actions help build and rebuild trust, making us feel a sense of security that the other person, truly, gets us. There's more on looping later in this chapter—it's a great strategy in conflicts.

> Finding your way through conflict requires engaging with some unhappy things, so fake attempts to reassure that "everything is going to be fine!" will corrode, not build, trust.

The second component of trust is a little trickier to understand initially. *Logic* simply means that trust requires that the other person makes sense to you, that their thinking is rigorous and sound. Someone nodding attentively and repeating back what you say with accuracy and affirmation will feel nice enough. But if they start describing the time that they sailed their ship off the edge of the flat earth, your trust is likely to break.

Finally, trust requires *authenticity*, which itself has two components: the authenticity of the other person and your own authenticity. Of course, you can only trust someone else if you feel that they are indeed being their authentic self, that they are showing up as the person that they really are. In conflict, our fraud radar is on high alert, and hucksters, manipulators, and other inauthentic sorts are certainly not going to gain our trust.

In early childhood settings, we have run into one particular form of inauthenticity over and over, and perhaps you have too. It's the happy-maker, the person who wants to put a smile on the faces of everyone else no matter their problems, concerns, or conflicts. Happy-makers create frustrating conflict narratives for their colleagues. And as you know now, finding your way through conflict requires engaging with some unhappy things, so fake attempts to reassure that "everything is going to be fine!" will corrode, not build, trust.

A relationship with a colleague who shows you empathy, makes sense, and seems genuine will feel trustworthy only if the empathy and understanding relates to your genuine self. Conversely, if you are forced to put up a façade at work because you feel unsafe or insecure, someone demonstrating empathy and understanding to your fake work-self might make you mistrust them.

So, trust requires empathy, logic, and authenticity. Each one is essential: you simply cannot fully trust someone in a situation that lacks any one of those components. Take a moment and ask yourself: to what extent do I trust my counterpart? Which of the three components feels relatively secure? Which seems unsteady or absent, and why?

Finally, how might you build up that shaky component to work through the conflict you're in? As it turns out, we have some helpful ideas about that!

Collaboration, Behavior Change, and Ambivalence

The first set of four strategies delineated in chapter 5 included individual homework for you to do without interacting with your counterpart. This second set of strategies is very intentionally collaborative.

That's for a good reason. In the midst of a conflict, you and your counterpart are likely to be quite lousy at doing anything remotely collaborative. You probably have been avoiding being in the same room whenever possible. So this second set of strategies involves seemingly simple collaborations that rely on explicit instructions and basic agreements. But don't be fooled: these collaborations may be small on paper, but they are mighty in practice.

> It's time to ask yourself the Big Question: *Do you really want to work out this conflict?*

To begin this collaboration, you need to take a vow to *front trust*. Conflict has shattered trust for you and your counterpart, and the last thing your defensive armor wants you to do is trust someone who has violated your sense of security. But that's what you're going to do: you are going to invest trust back into the relationship.

You'll start with small doses of trust, ones that set the stage for the actual conversation you'll have soon. Don't worry if you feel suspicious—that's a likely response given the situation. If it feels too difficult to invest trust in the person, then tweak your vow and front trust into the process itself. Believe us, it works.

It works, that is, if what you really want to do is resolve this conflict.

If you feel hesitant as you read this chapter, if your commitment to initiating this collaboration feels shaky, if you list lots of reasons why each step is difficult or impossible, if you find yourself putting the book down a lot to do other things, it's time to ask yourself the Big Question: *Do you really want to work out this conflict?*

Do you truly want to change the relationship you have with your counterpart? Do you actually want to do the individual and collaborative work necessary to rebuild trust? Is a working relationship, built on a genuinely respectful engagement with this flawed human being, your goal?

We ask this question because many workshop participants tell us that their situation is different than others, more challenging and complicated. Truth be told, the conflicts they describe are just like those we've been discussing. But they don't want to hear that. Instead, they want to tell us all the reasons that the other person is wrong.

After dozens of these sorts of protests, we've come to the conclusion that some people simply don't want to solve their stated conflicts. They resist the idea that they'll have to create new, trustworthy, respectful relationships with those very people.

In our attempt to sort out what this all means, we turned our attention to the research on adult behavior change. Specifically, we examined the technique of motivational interviewing used by social workers and psychologists, and it helped us to understand why these attitudes seem so powerful. We learned that whenever an adult wants to change their behavior, their perspective is shaped by deep and powerful ambivalence. This ambivalence is a healthy, normal part of human behavior.

For an example, let's assume that, like both of us, you at some point in your life have wanted to lose a bit of weight. The plan is simple enough—modify your diet, reduce caloric intake, get more exercise—and when you announce your New Year's resolution to friends and family, you state your attitude shift clearly and confidently. But a few days later in the checkout line you once again grab that bag of chips or cookies, convincing yourself in the car ride home that it's no big deal. A month down the road, your scale shows no improvement, and you start telling yourself that it's just not going to work and isn't worth the trouble. Your ambivalence is revealing itself all the while.

The technique of motivational interviewing involves engaging with this ambivalence. Eating the unplanned snack is familiar. Slipping back into old behavior, you cut yourself some slack. After all, you've been eating this way for a long time. Throughout the difficult process of change, you're going to keep being the very person who has sustained the behavior you declared you wanted to change.

But the sustaining behavior and slip-ups in the plan don't mean that you no longer desire to change. They're there because you do. Your very attempts to change activate these sustaining thoughts and feelings; they are part and parcel of real behavior change. So give yourself some support when you exhibit these predictable human traits.

The question, "Do you really want to work out this conflict?" often produces this same sort of ambivalence between change and sustain attitudes. "Of course I want to work more effectively with my classroom partner instead of bringing the same problems home every night!" is a perfect example of a sincere, legitimate change attitude. But don't be surprised if some old, bad habits resurface in the form of repeated grievances and blame, bad habits that reveal that you're still sustaining some attitudes and behaviors at the same time. Holding a commitment to change while experiencing the same old obstacles to that change reveals your ambivalence—and is a perfectly typical reaction to this sort of behavior change.

That ambivalence presents you with exactly two options. The easy way out is sustaining the behavior and attitudes that you've built up toward your counterpart and deciding you're not going to change. Of course, this "way out" keeps you in conflict.

The better, harder way out requires that you accept your ambivalence as a predictable human trait. Make your peace with it, for it's unlikely to go away any time soon. As you do, recognize sustaining behaviors and attitudes for what they are, symptoms of your desire to change, not the proof that you cannot. Don't give them too much energy or attention.

Instead, give that energy and attention to change-based attitudes and behaviors. Cultivate them actively. Tell your squad or village about your plan and recruit their support for it. Imagine a world in which the change has happened, with all of its relief and benefit. Celebrate each success in the process.

And pat yourself on the back for the effort. Initiating a collaboration with your counterpart will require that courage we mentioned earlier. But now you're good at doing the slightly scary stuff, right?

Collaboration 1: Figure Out Logistics

As we've discussed throughout the book, conflict produces strange logic when it comes to the "little stuff." One misstep can stand in for an entire personality as "proof" that your suspicions have been right all along. A missing piece of art means disrespect; a poorly timed scowl means hate.

Nowhere is this truer than in the logistics of setting the stage for conflict resolution. A poorly timed meeting, held in the wrong place and focused on an unclear agenda, is a recipe for making the conflict much worse, not better. Instead of feeling like you're able to figure out the problem, the problem expands to include the impossibility of working together on even the "simple stuff."

So that means you have to collaborate on the logistics. Remember all that hard work that Chris put into planning his meeting with that frustrated parent? It backfired because he wasn't collaborative; he designed each and every detail of the logistics on his own. So no matter how wonderful he thought his agenda was, to the parent it was proof that he had his own ulterior motives.

You are going to learn from his mistakes. Instead of becoming the expert on conflict and imposing your expertise on your counterpart, you're going to work out each detail in dialogue, recognizing that there are no experts within this particular conflict. In doing so, you'll begin the process of fronting and thus building trust.

Clarify the Topic by Agreeing on What You're Going to Discuss

"We need to talk": those four words can make one's heart race and palms sweat. It doesn't matter if your parent, your partner, or your colleague says it. Regardless of the speaker, it suggests a creeping, scary disaster is looming.

It's also an unfair, manipulative, and counterproductive lie.

It's a lie because, as you probably have thought when hearing it once or twice, "*We* don't need to talk. *You* need to talk! I don't!" One person stating it to another attempts a manipulation, sticking the "we" where "I" belongs. It puts the other person in an unfair situation that, whatever the intent, is just wrong.

It's also stunningly counterproductive. Over and over we have watched participants start their Robin and Pat discussions with vague, scary openers. "So I'm kind of wondering if we can chat a bit about something." "Do you think we could talk about what happened?" "Hey! I was hoping we'd run into each other so, you know, we might, like . . ." Those questions and hesitant statements make it clear that, at least in our profession, we adults could learn a lot from young children about stating our truths.

Let's do a reset. You're in a conflict. Trust is broken. Details matter. And you're going to take the first steps toward modeling the way through the conflict by being courageous and specific.

It's surprisingly easy to create a fair, straightforward, productive statement of truth. Feeling some tension related to scheduling? Then say, "I'm feeling some tension related to scheduling and want to talk about it with you." Unsure what happened in the hallway last week with that parent and feeling shaken by it? Then say, "I'm unsure what happened in the hallway last week with you and feel a bit shaken by it. I'd like to find time to talk about it."

"I" statements that declare an honest, straightforward truth about the conflict are easy to write, hard to say out loud, and, nearly always, a terrific relief for both speaker and listener. They are easy to write if you simply state, from your perspective, what the objective facts are: something happened; it had an impact on you; you want to talk about it. They are hard to say out loud because it often feels like you're violating social norms by being specific about a problem. (That's why "We need to talk" was invented!)

But, trust us, "I" statements are almost always a relief for both parties. For the speaker, you're finally letting that thought that has been bouncing around in your head for days or weeks see the light of day. It's a relief to acknowledge its reality. Most of the time your statement is a relief to the listener as well. They've been wondering what happened to disrupt your relationship; things have seemed strained and tense to them and they aren't sure why.

Finally, these simple, straightforward sentences declare something crucial about your relationship. They state that there is a problem to work out together, which means that *the problem is not the other person.* By fronting trust that you can name, figure out, and work through a conflict, you are telling your counterpart that the misstep, error, or confusion is the problem, and not them. Stating what the problem is also declares who the problem is not.

So take your "I" statement very seriously. Write it down. Practice saying it to your bedroom mirror or a friend. Get it just right. Put the work into this crucial first step.

When you deliver the statement, recognize that, if things go well, your counterpart may decide to share one (or twenty) "I" statements of their own. That is the ideal reaction: you've named something that's not only important to you but also important to them, and they are eager to share their thoughts. It could go so well that you're tempted to just dive in right there.

Don't dive in. Stop. You have more planning to do.

Choose the Right Location

There is a glorious moment that has happened now and then in our careers as school leaders, a rare but heartwarming event. We walk into a classroom where the two teachers have had their issues over the months or years and see a team that has learned how to work through their conflicts with panache, good humor, and skill. It goes something like this.

It's a chilly November day in Michigan. Preschool co-teachers DJ and Nev are prompting children to get ready to go outside. DJ grew up in the region and is used to the cold. Meanwhile, Nev comes from the south and hasn't gotten used to the frigid weather. Here's how their instructions to the children unfold.

Nev: "Okay everyone! You need your snow pants, boots, a hat, and mittens."

DJ: "Nev, do you really think that they need snow pants? There's no snow on the ground."

Nev: "Yeah, I do. I think it's supposed to be pretty cold today, isn't it?"

DJ: "Well, yesterday it was 45 degrees—pretty warm for Michigan in November—and today it's supposed to be the same. But let's check the weather to be sure."

Reaching for the classroom tablet, Nev opens the weather app and reads, "Yup, the current temp is 30 degrees, and the windchill is 18 degrees. Brrr."

DJ: "Brrrr is right! I'm going to wear my snow pants too. I'm glad you said something—unpredictable Michigan weather."

Seems pretty simple, right? Let's unpack this conflict to see why it worked out so well. Indeed, it worked out so well you may be wondering, "What conflict?"

The first and biggest component of the conflict is the one that preschool children need to witness over and over again for their social and emotional development. From the outset, Nev and DJ respectfully, calmly disagree. There's no grumbling, no passive-aggressive "There she goes again about the snow pants" complaints.

Instead of going silent when the difference of opinion is clear, they speak the conflict out loud. They take turns sharing their perspectives, briefly explaining the reasons for their thoughts. Their goal isn't to prove the other one wrong; rather, their goal is to gather and share information to reach a reasonable outcome.

What's more, they are keenly aware that they are in a classroom with children who are listening. Instead of treating the conflict as a problem, it's an opportunity to teach. For example, Nev and DJ model problem-solving. When they realize that they don't have all the information that they need, they grab their tablet and look up the temperature. When that information is different from the forecast, they abandon their previous basis for decision-making and use a more accurate one, accommodating the new information and adjusting their actions in kind.

We want children to have repeated opportunities to develop the skill of being in conflict by watching the adults who care for them do so.

Finally and most importantly, the children witness a conflict between two people they know and trust from start to finish. They get to observe a relationship teeter and then steady itself—rupture and repair in one easy exchange about snow pants. They are taught in the most efficient manner, watching two adults with whom they have an attachment perform the social development skills that all children and adults need.

In these situations, the classroom is the ideal place for adults to work out conflicts. Too often conflicts start in front of children only to be resolved away from them. To be sure, that is sometimes necessary: when the content is inappropriate or too nuanced for young children, or our reactive emotions prevent us from modeling with calm and care. However, doing so means that children see only the conflict erupt and not the process of resolution. We want children to have repeated opportunities to develop the skill of being in conflict by watching the adults who care for them do so. DJ and Nev's classroom is lucky enough to see the whole process.

It's glorious, isn't it? Unfortunately, it's all too rare. Instead, this sort of thing is more likely to happen.

Jion and Li are co-teachers in a toddler classroom. Li is relatively new; Jion has been working there for years. Licensing requires them to change children's diapers every two hours. When their education coordinator met with them, they created a rotating schedule that they follow fairly regularly.

However, everything breaks down when a child needs a change in between the scheduled times, and today is no different. While Li is dancing with a few children, Jion sits across the room with Emmi, sniffs the air, and makes a face.

Jion: "Looks like Emmi needs a diaper change."

Li scowls at Jion and keeps dancing. Jion stares and repeats, "Did you hear? Emmi needs a change."

Li stops dancing and shuts off the music. "Yes, I heard you! Come here, Emmi. Let me change you."

As Emmi crosses the room to the changing table, Li sighs. "Every time someone poops, you never volunteer to do it!" Li grabs Emmi under the arms and plops her onto the table, starting the changing process.

Jion laughs. "Give me a break. I mean, is it going to kill you?"

What a toxic mess—and we don't mean what's happening in Emmi's diaper!

First of all, though the intent of Li and Jion's complaining is directed at each other, they are in a classroom filled with children whose healthy narcissism will make them assume that the teachers are talking about them. That means that the impact of this dialogue is likely to shame children, and specifically poor Emmi, for their biological needs. She's too young to understand the complexity of the situation, for sure, but Emmi's not wrong to believe that her requiring a diaper change makes teachers angry.

Young children are dependent on early childhood professionals to have their needs met. Treating their needs as an inconvenience is profoundly disrespectful and damaging to their developing body knowledge and self-esteem. In addition, young children don't understand sarcasm, so Jion's response about Li dying from a diaper change makes the situation sound much more dire than it actually is.

So, while Emmi's diaper does indeed get changed and the disagreement between Li and Jion flows back in time, the event produces sustained tension that continues on. After all, Emmi isn't the last child to require a change of a diaper "off schedule," and the underlying frustration between Li and Jion will likely resurface each time the situation repeats. When it does, the teachers will again produce a model for toxic behavior, demonstrating that uncomfortable emotions and petty grievances are the norm for these two adults.

Until Li and Jion develop the skills that Nev and DJ have built, they need to work out their conflicts in a place where there are no children around. They are likely to fumble about, modeling the opposite of the behavior we want children to experience. That's okay—like the rest of us, they aren't perfect—but the classroom is the wrong place for that fumbling.

So what is a good place? Once again, there's no single definition of "good place," so you have some questions to answer in collaboration with your counterpart. You can start by saying, "I wonder if this conversation would be easier if we waited until we are in a space separate from children?" or "I think we could both focus better on communicating clearly if we had this discussion outside of the classroom."

Start by figuring out whether you both prefer to meet inside the workplace or out in a public space like a coffee shop or library. Are you more comfortable being in public in this situation? Or do you want to stay in the building? You can simply say to your counterpart, "Where would you be most comfortable having this conversation?"

Next, think about privacy and confidentiality. We strongly urge you to be in a place where no one else can hear what you're saying, which could be a buzzy food court or other public space. In our experience, however, folks want to stay at work—and that presents a problem. "I want to respect your feelings and privacy, so let's go somewhere where we can be sure we can express our perspectives without someone overhearing and taking things out of context."

Ask yourself, is there a truly private space in your workplace? We've worked in buildings that had rooms with rolling partitions, which certainly don't provide the sound barrier that floor-to-ceiling walls provide. Sitting off at one end of a large room doesn't work well either—voices carry, especially when two people are in a juicy mess. So if at all possible try to find a room that ensures you won't be heard. If not, consider a white noise machine or app for your cell phone, which you can turn on just outside the room you'll be in.

Finally, think hard about how visible you want your discussion to be. Chances are pretty good that other folks would love to swing by and "see how you're doing," but that's a bad idea. Rooms surrounded by glass are like stages, and you probably don't want an audience for this situation. If the only option involves glass you can't cover with curtains or blinds, agree to turn your backs to the windows.

Schedule a Time for the Conversation to Occur

Let's recall one of the core principles from the introduction: conflict is the work, not a distraction from the work. You'll want to keep that principle in mind as you sort out this critical step.

As you probably know, most other professionals do not work in organizations that demand that they stay in one room for hours at a time, unable to take a break, with only a few duties outside the room. The requirement that early childhood educators maintain teacher:child ratios in their classroom is one of the biggest causes of conflict in our profession. If we accept that conflict is the work, then we also have to accept that the work requires coverage.

Coverage is hard to find. Most programs we know about are short-staffed, and getting someone in the room to meet, much less exceed, ratio is a daily grind for management. What's more, most administrators don't see conflict resolution as a work problem requiring coverage—you should just figure it out on your own, right?

These constraints mean that, more often than not, educators are expected to take care of conflicts as soon as they pop up and as quickly as possible. Moreover, being humans who don't like conflict, we often want to solve things in the heat of the moment, hoping to fix the problem right away so that we extinguish the discomfort of our overwhelming emotions and shattered trust immediately. Of course, reactivity is our enemy, and diving right into the problem almost always amplifies the tension. And, as we discussed above, working out your trickiest conflicts with colleagues in classrooms is rarely a good idea for the children in our care.

So, working together, you are going to agree upon an appropriate time to have the conversation. And there is usually no rush. A high school basketball coach once told us about his twenty-four-hour rule: he is happy to talk with any parent about any issue related to their child's performance or his coaching during a game—but no earlier than twenty-four hours after the game has ended. Though many conflicts, by their nature, feel tremendously urgent, we think the coach has a good point. Time doesn't heal or solve problems, but it does give us distance from the heat of the moment and thus more time to respond instead of react.

Inserting a delay in even the most urgent situations is almost always a good idea. Several years ago, Christine was a toddler teacher at a large child care center with a child who had severe allergies. One day, the center cook mistakenly prepared something that contained the allergen for that child. When Christine confronted the cook about it immediately, it was a tense and unproductive conversation, as the cook defensively denied the error in preparation.

But Christine then separated the urgent part from the rest. Pausing the heated conversation, she simply chose not to serve the food to the child, avoiding the dangerous situation without rushing to resolve the conflict with the cook. Later that day, outside of the classroom, during teacher planning time, and after the children had gone down for nap, Christine approached the cook to start the process.

Ask yourself and your counterpart when the "appropriate" time would be to have the conversation. Does the situation dictate a fairly rapid resolution due to pending decisions or requirements? Can you put the conflict on hold while returning to other aspects of your collaboration? Does one of you need some time to sort it out, or does one of you feel a sense of urgency? While overwhelming emotions urge you to solve the problem, it's a favor to all if one of you can say, "Is this the best time to solve the problem?" or "I propose we table this until we've both had time to gather our thoughts."

Finally, as with most of these logistics, be prepared to compromise. You're in a conflict, and chances are good that some of these negotiations will reveal stark differences. If you can front trust into the process and make accommodations for your counterpart, it's a lot more likely that they'll start to do the same for you, easing the way through the conflict resolution process ahead.

That said, there is one scheduling matter that you won't compromise on. It's such a big deal that it has its own section.

Collaboration 2: Plan for Plenty of Time

The only thing you can predict about the length of time you'll need to work on and resolve this conflict is that it's unpredictable. We've watched conflicts unfold over months and months, only to have the resolution take three minutes. And we've watched sudden, "little" conflicts pop up that require hours to address.

You may think that you know how much time you need, but that's just your initial response to your own perspective. You don't know the other person's perspective yet—and you don't know how you'll react when you do.

So we strongly urge you to plan for plenty of time. Here's why.

Empathy Takes Time

Remember Frances Frei's insistence that all three components of trust—empathy, logic, and authenticity—must be present? Since your main goal is to rebuild shattered trust, you both need sufficient time to ensure that things make sense, that you can see the other person's perspective, and that you and your counterpart have truly shown up. The process itself creates a space for authenticity, and the strategy of looping, with its focus on objective reporting and acknowledgment, supports logic.

And empathy? Well, that's a bit more complicated when you're in conflict. As Frei explains, empathy is "the most common wobble," because conflict has activated all of our self-preserving defensives (Frei 2018). Since we are what Frei calls "too self-distracted," we need time both to understand another's perspective and feelings and to articulate our own in a comprehensible manner. Empathy takes work, and that work takes focus. We live in a fast-paced world in which we are expected to multi-task, juggling multiple responsibilities and balancing distraction and attention.

Empathy takes work, and that work takes focus.

Like the sustaining thoughts that fly through your head when you're trying to change your behavior, those distractions should be noticed and then released. Frei encourages us to handle our distractions by getting to know them a bit better, identifying where, with, and to whom or what you are likely to offer your distraction. Your job in preparing for conflict resolution is to do all that you can to eliminate those distractions—to-do lists, family members, cell phones, nosy colleagues—so you have the time and the ability to be present with the person or people with whom you are in conflict.

Slow. Down.

Many of us are out of the habit of focusing our attention on a single situation. And nearly all of us have forgotten what it means to slow down. Way, way down.

As discussed in chapter 4 when examining Robin and Pat's conflict, one of the key elements of the role play is the absurdly short amount of time we allow to resolve the conflict in workshop settings. A few minutes is just enough for participants to react, not respond strategically, so they are using all of their least useful skills. And that means that they typically dive in by declaring how they feel or what happened to them, building defensiveness and extinguishing any possible space for developing empathy.

So it's time to slow down, not hurry up. Immersing yourself in someone else's perspective has to flow naturally. You need time to let yourself truly perceive the other person, and time for them to truly see you.

Steps to Help You Slow Down and Plan for Time

1. First and foremost, during your planning, discuss together how much time you anticipate you will need—and be sure not to rush this detail. It may seem like a quick conversation

to you, but your counterpart may have a very different take. We strongly suggest that you anticipate more time than you expect you'll need to work through the situation and feel like trust has been restored.

2. Then, once you have a shared sense of how long it will take, double it. If you agree that it should take about 30 minutes, schedule it for an hour. If you think it will take an hour, schedule two. The extra time may or may not be needed for the conversation, but if it's not, you'll be able to meet without rushing in and out of it.

3. Now that you have a plan for how long you need, consider whether it makes sense to break the conversation in two. Given that time is in short supply in early childhood settings, it's possible that you won't be able to carve out a full hour or two at one time. So instead of shortening your conversation, plan to pause at half time and return a little bit later when you can.

4. During the conversation itself, it's important to go slowly, taking time to pause as needed. If you do have to break your discussion in two, allow time at the end of the first part to recap what has happened, regroup, and decide on next steps. Then do something similar at the start of the next session, recapping what happened and stating what you hope to accomplish.

5. During your meeting, be alert to the desire to rush to a conclusion or to hurry through something thorny. That desire is very real and very powerful, and you'll feel the tug of distractions that will make rushing seem like a good idea. It's not.

6. Finally, reassure yourself that you are not, in fact, taking time. You are investing it. Think of the dozens or hundreds of hours you have spent avoiding, worrying about, getting angry over, and otherwise unproductively dealing with this conflict. The hour or two you invest here will pay off for weeks and months to come.

Collaboration 3: Clarify Shared Expectations

We rarely meet folks who recognize the critical importance of clarifying shared expectations. But finding your way through the conflict requires figuring out the ground rules for the discussion. One of the expectations that you both are likely to identify is "We do not share several important expectations, so we will have to deal with that first."

Considering the complexities of personality, culture, meaning, and context in any given situation, conflict is very likely to reveal a fundamental lack of alignment between you and your counterpart. Thus, to ground this strategy, we return to the notion of fronting trust. However, the discussion about shared expectations may well challenge the tentative trust you've fronted, for you, for them, or for you both.

So a first, crucial expectation requires committing to "good-enough trust." You are too early in the process to lean into a deep and abiding trust, one requiring the empathy, logic, and authenticity you have yet to rebuild. At this stage, you need to establish good-enough trust with each other, an explicit promise to front some preliminary trust that will allow you to get the collaborative work off the ground. And good-enough trust still requires all three components of trust, but in different portions: a bit of empathy, a good dose of authenticity—and a hefty serving of logic.

Good-enough trust among early childhood education colleagues often sounds like, "I know we are both equally committed to supporting families" or "I know we both prioritize children's needs." These kinds of statements can bring down walls that prevent problem-solving because when they are said to us, we feel seen and valued. And when we say them to others, we aren't giving anything of ourselves away—we can be authentic and front trust.

The logic portion of this is where it gets a little tricky. Remember how we just said there needs to be a hefty amount of logic? It's going to take a lot of solid reasoning to work through difficulty. But despite our best reasoning, logic is sometimes wobblier than we expect it to be; in fact, it can be quite fragile. Frei describes the fragility of logic as having two parts: quality of logic and your ability to communicate (Frei 2018). The logic must make sense; your logic has to be logical! So it's only strong if it is based on solid reasoning. Sometimes our assessment of our reasoning can be skewed by our emotional reaction and intense attachment to our perspective. But just as important as reasoning, you need the ability to communicate your logic in a manner that can be easily understood within this conflict. Given our reactivity, that can be a challenge.

Luckily for us, our field has a number of organizations that have given time and thought to guide us through conflict and help us communicate logically. The frameworks that follow can be used as talking points for your organization and with your counterpart when creating shared ground rules to discuss the conflict. In addition, a shared commitment to such frameworks is impersonal and objective, centered on broader principles or expectations and not mired in the specific details of the conflict at hand.

Mission, Vision, and Values Statements

Most early childhood education organizations have mission, vision, and values statements. Very few organizations reference these statements routinely, and we think that's a mistake. Generally, they are helpful for establishing shared principles for collaborative work, and when things get dicey, they provide excellent means by which you can step back and view a situation with greater perspective.

If you're lucky, the best mission, vision, and values statements are those in your workplace. But in case you don't have them on hand, here are a few examples of mission statements from high-quality early childhood education organizations providing direct care to children and families.

Gretchen's House strives to provide a high quality Early Childhood Program by creating a safe, healthy, and nurturing environment that promotes the physical, social, emotional, and cognitive development of young children and responds to the needs of families. Our parents and staff are partners, working together to meet the needs of the children and their families. As partners, we will communicate regularly and thoughtfully with each other to build a relationship of trust and respect (Gretchen's House 2019).

The Goddard School uses the most current, academically endorsed methods to ensure that children have fun while learning the skills they need for long-term success in school and in life. Our talented teachers also collaborate with parents to nurture children into respectful, confident and joyful learners (Goddard School 2020).

The Bright Horizons Family Solutions mission is to provide innovative programs that help children, families, and employers work together to be their very best. We are committed to providing the highest quality child-care, early education, and work/life solutions in the nation. We strive to: nurture each child's unique qualities and potential; support families through strong partnerships; collaborate with employers to build family friendly workplaces; create a work environment that encourages professionalism, growth, and diversity; grow a financially strong organization. We aspire to do this so successfully that we make a difference in the lives of children and families and in the communities where we live and work (Bright Horizons 2020).

When we collaborate to address a conflict, mission statements like these allow us to ask important questions about both intent and impact. Which statements resonate more or less with each person? To what extent do our actions in this situation foster relationships of attachment with children and trust and respect with families? In what ways did our response in conflict contribute to an ethos of professionalism in our organization?

These and other questions don't need to be answered definitively. Rather, they are provocations, prompts toward more intentional moments of reflection that attend to your commitment to children and each other with humility and focus. While it can be tricky to engage those questions in collaboration, we heartily encourage you to try to do so.

Job Descriptions and Employee Handbooks

It is shocking to both of us that very few people engage in workplace conflict resolution by referring to the documents that describe their roles within that workplace. Job descriptions are built precisely to describe the work you should do in the position for which you are paid; employee handbooks describe the expectations for all employees set by the organization that pays you for that work. In a workplace conflict, they are the legal, administrative, actionable documents that probably structure the majority of the conflict's content. They are, in short, essential.

Your first order of business is to find out exactly what your organization has on hand. Talk to your supervisor or the head of human resources, and ask them to give you all of the relevant job descriptions and any pertinent portions of the employee handbook. Then sit down and review them carefully. Don't feel too bad if this is the first time you've reviewed them, or if they seem utterly unfamiliar. After all, such expectations can be hard for staff to implement since employees rarely have opportunities to understand and internalize documents that are simply handed to them at orientation to be signed and filed.

That said, you're likely to find that the language used in the documents includes useful ways to articulate your thoughts. That language clarifies the roles and responsibilities you both agreed to fulfill when you accepted your jobs. Of course, no matter how objectively they are written, interpretation will vary. Similar to mission statements, many phrases in early childhood education job descriptions are icebergs. What exactly do terms like *high-quality*, *developmentally appropriate*, *emergent learning*, and *differentiation* mean in the real, messy world of practice? And who gets to decide what employment expectations like *cooperation*, *mutual respect*, and *diligence* actually look like?

As a result, it's important to approach a discussion about job-related documents as a collaborative exercise in interpretation. Together, you can try to identify the key concepts at stake in the conflict—without moving to interpret, judge, or blame each other's actions. That's an important warning, one that you'll want to make clear when you suggest to your counterpart that these documents could help you both out.

And while you're doing that, stress that you're putting your trust in the process and the other person, not initiating a job action with the documents at hand. Chances are your counterpart has never looked carefully at any of them, after all, and it would be rather alarming for you to suddenly stick them under their nose. So reassure your counterpart that, like the other guidelines in this chapter, these documents are intended to support your collaboration, not supplant it.

A Group Agreement

In our workshops, when we bring up the topic of job descriptions and employee handbooks, there are always a few participants who smile and shake their heads. "Wishful thinking," they tell us. "I sure would like to work at an organization that took the time to clarify those expectations for me." So, if you happen to work for an employer that hasn't taken care of those basic organizational expectations, you have another option: establish your own group agreement. It sounds daunting, but it can be very simple—and still very powerful and useful.

Ideally, this group agreement would include everyone at the organization, or at least a subset of people who are working as a team in some way within it. However, it's also possible for you to create a shared agreement with just two members: you and your counterpart. We use the process that follows to establish group agreements, which you can modify to fit your particular situation.

The group agreement is exactly what it sounds like: a basic, staff-developed, and agreed-upon way of working together. Like everything in this chapter, it can only work as a collaboration, developed with the individuals who are impacted by the work it describes. It is not, therefore, a list of rules and regulations handed down from boss to workers. Rather, the function of leadership is to facilitate the collaborative engagement truly effective agreements require.

That takes buy-in. People are much more likely to agree to something if it is written in their words and developed from their ideas, thereby reflecting themselves and their priorities. A group agreement is best created at the onset of work together and is meant to be a living document, reviewed as you work together over time, modified as it becomes apparent that any necessary "rules of engagement" have been overlooked.

Christine recently became the center director of a program with over fifty teachers and support staff, and establishing a group agreement was the very first conversation they had as a whole team. A mission statement already existed, but Christine knew that she was taking over for a director who had served for many years and their leadership styles differed. Taking the time to establish a group agreement helped everyone with the transition to Christine's leadership style.

Support
Have Fun
Be Flexible
Accept Imperfections
Recognize Differences
Assume Good Intentions
Respect Individuality
Take Responsibility
Communicate
Encourage
Help

As a whole team, they explored their values and renewed their shared commitment for how they were going to work together successfully. Next, they created a visual poster (as seen on page 111) with their words of commitment to one another and posted it all over the center.

The key to success in creating this type of staff-developed, living agreement is to push past abstraction to concrete indicators, asking people to explain exactly what they mean by the terms they offer. People always want to use words or phrases like *communicate, respect, listen,* and so on, but as we've detailed earlier in the book, those icebergs don't help much. So the facilitator needs to nudge people forward with clarifying questions that require further definition and explanation. The questions have two benefits: they require people to slow down and envision these qualities, not only how each person embodies them but also how they experience those qualities in others; and they require people to recognize that words mean different things to different people. Unless the facilitator poses these questions, people will make different assumptions about what the group is agreeing to, creating greater tension rather than less.

This agreement is useful to establish a foundation of shared expectations, in staff's own words, about how to exist together. Specifically, in conflict situations, it can be useful for each person involved in the conflict to consider if their words and actions align with the commitment they made to one another.

The NAEYC Code of Ethics

When we present this content at a workshop, participants regularly ask us questions about colleagues who refuse to cooperate in the conflict resolution process. "What do you do with someone who just won't participate in productive discussion?" "How do you handle teachers who implement developmentally *in*appropriate activities for children?" "But what about people who keep doing one thing even when you've agreed to something else?" Of course conflict resolution is much easier when people are actively engaged and genuinely working to implement the strategies. When working with people who engage otherwise, you have a few different options.

You could simply ask, "What's up?" and try to understand their perspective. This open-ended inquiry can go several different directions, some good, others really bad. Tone, timing, and intention could muddy the space for conflict resolution even more.

So it's good to have other options that are not individualized for the employee in question but draw from preexisting professional resources that emphasize consistency, process, and transparency. If you are a supervisor, it's smart to take the issue to your human resources department if the issues include failure to comply with licensing regulations, excessive absenteeism, or breaking confidentiality with child or family information. These types of performance-based issues need to be addressed with specific legal processes or a professional improvement plan from human resources.

If the HR option is untenable—and even if your HR department is solid—we urge you to incorporate the National Association for the Education of Young Children (NAEYC) Code of Ethics into regular practice and discussion. The NAEYC Code of Ethics differs from job descriptions or value-setting conversations in that it provides general professional expectations for early childhood educators in four categories: children, families, colleagues, and the community (NAEYC 2011). While the language of the Code is general, it provides objective, neutral, and clear expectations that can be easily discussed and used for context in conflict situations, focusing on the work rather than our opinions.

We have found that framing conflict by bringing the impact on children to the fore is essential.

Most importantly, the NAEYC Code of Ethics helps keep conversations child-focused. Our responsibility in our professional roles as educators is to care for and advocate on behalf of children and their families. That's what we are paid to do. However, as we've seen over and over, children are often erased in workplace conflicts, the innocent bystanders of adult ignorance or mistreatment.

We have found that framing conflict by bringing the impact on children to the fore is essential, and the NAEYC Code of Ethics is the best tool we know of to do that. The Code is most effective when you and your team have established it as a structuring framework for the organization well in advance of the conflict in question, enabling all parties to explore it with a clear mind and commit to its principles.

Christine established the Code as the ethical foundation for her new team's work together because of its power to create the basis of a group's ethics and behavior before specific conflicts arise. In their second conversation, the team spent two hours dissecting the language and coming up with examples of what the Code of Ethics statements look like (and don't look like) in practice. Together, the group agreement and the NAEYC Code of Ethics formed the foundation for their professional work.

If you don't have these contexts in place in your setting, it's not too late! Start now. If you have them but it's been a while, dust them off and bring them back to the conversation. After all, it is impossible for people to meet expectations if they don't know what they are, and it's unfair to boot. And you don't have to be the formal organizational leader to initiate either conversation. It's the right thing for anyone to do.

Collaboration 4: Establish a Safe and Neutral Ground

In her TED Talk on trust, Frei addresses "the leaders in the room" directly, declaring that "it is your obligation to set the conditions that not only make it safe for us to be authentic but makes it welcome. Makes it celebrated" (Frei 2018). Leaders and people in positions of power have both an opportunity and responsibility to model this authentic way of being through intentional use of their power and resources. While there are multiple ways to perform and utilize power, this strategy focuses on physical space and logistics.

In every workplace there are subtle factors that contribute to employees' sense of safety, factors that enable or prevent productive conflict engagement. These factors are intensified when one person has more power than the other within an organization, and particularly when one person supervises another. Given the frequency of these sorts of workplace conflicts between manager and employee, this fourth element of collaboration is largely the responsibility of the supervisor.

Meeting in the director's office versus meeting in a shared, neutral space can have a big impact on how the conversation goes. Likewise, style of furniture, proximity of seating, and positioning of seating are all environmental factors that contribute to power dynamics and therefore require very intentional decisions. When Christine started her new job as a center director, she found herself faced with a lot of them.

When I began in my new position, many tasks needed my attention. However, I immediately realized that there was one task that couldn't wait: I needed to change my office.

I inherited the office from a long-time director, and I could tell that her presence was baked into the walls and floor and furniture. During her tenure, the office arrangement made sense for her and the staff. But I wasn't her and the mismatch wasn't building trust. Also, I have a very strong visual sense, and I could tell that there were several relationship-damaging elements in the office that had to be addressed before I was going to build trust with anyone on my new team.

First, the fixed computer desk was positioned such that I was required to sit with my back to the door to my office. I knew that to every visitor, seeing my back would immediately send the message that I wasn't available—that my desk work was more important than them. I was able to make an internal furniture swap for a new desk that faced the door, giving me the chance to smile and make eye contact with anyone that walked by.

Next, there were limited seating options in my office. To most people, the director's desk chair and a comfy couch wouldn't present an issue. But I quickly realized three big problems. The director's chair—a genuine power seat—was slightly taller than the couch. With no other seating options, that meant that sitting in my chair would place me above any seated visitor. Also, the single couch meant that people who were upset with each other had to share the same physical space, possibly even touching, which increased vulnerability for people already beset by their big emotions. Finally, the couch made it very difficult for people sitting shoulder-to-shoulder to see each other and make eye contact. The couch made it too easy for people to avoid facing each other both physically and metaphorically.

Time for new furniture! I replaced the couch with two equally comfy chairs, both of which are slightly angled to face each other but easily moved when needed. When I have a conversation in my office, I get up from my director's chair and sit with the visitor in the comfy chairs. Now we are even in height, style, and position, thereby leveraging a conversation of even contribution. As a result, there's no "power seat" in the room during discussions, and there's flexibility for people to position themselves to comfortably be in conversation.

Next up: where was the space for collaborative work? The only flat work surface in the room was my desk, implying that my individual work was more important than anything we could do collaboratively. Along with the other features, this made the space available only for necessary, one-sided conversations. To remedy this, I added a working table with a chair on either side, and a bulletin board above for planning and strategizing. In addition to the comfy chairs, this is a second option for conversation, allowing people to choose the most optimal dynamic for working through a situation. And the two table chairs—the same height and style as the new comfy duo—allow additional visitors to join a conversation at the same level.

Finally, the office in general was dark and cluttered, creating an atmosphere that no one wanted to be in and from which everyone fled as quickly as possible. Did I want to give a sense of my own personality and style? Of course! But the decorative priority was lighting and organization. I removed every unnecessary thing I could and added light-colored furniture, some plants, and a few inspiring trinkets and fidgets to be played with.

I'll be honest with you: when I started making changes to my office, I heard murmurings of people annoyed and concerned that I was shallow and materialistic, only wanting to spend my time on decor. But then people started spending time in my new office, saying things like, "Wow, I just want to come in here and hang out" and "It feels so comfortable in here." "What a difference!" one person said. "I don't even know how to describe it." That, of course, was exactly my goal.

Once it was set up, I stopped spending time in it. I made it available to other people in my building. And I prioritized time in other spaces to vary my interactions with my staff. Meanwhile, they started holding conferences in there, using it for private work, holding team meetings, and so on. I made it clear that it was for everyone.

I do work at my desk from time to time and meet with people in my office when necessary, but these steps completely shifted the atmosphere of the space. It wasn't a room of fear and dread—it became a room of trust and collaboration. So when we do have to have difficult conversations (and believe me, we do!), the atmosphere filled with familiar feelings of trust and collaboration is woven into our conversation.

These environmental changes made significant positive differences to the workspace and tone for challenging conversations, enabling each person to come to the conversation feeling safe. As you can see in Christine's situation, these changes were pivotal to building and rebuilding trust, an important step to creating a successful team able to engage productively and respectfully in conflict resolution.

While this strategy is primarily for leaders and supervisors, it can be helpful for everyone to consider. You may not be able to make significant changes to a conversation space like Christine did, but carefully considering where you choose to meet can alleviate some stress. Likewise, respecting individual physical boundaries and being on the same physical level can reduce some tension in a conflict conversation. If you're not sure, it's okay to simply ask yourself and the other person, "Does this feel like a safe and neutral space for a conversation?" If the answer is no, you can collaborate on some adjustments. It's worth the time you put into this to make it possible for both people to fully engage in the conversation.

Do Not Skip These Steps!

The intentional practices discussed in this chapter matter because they change the trajectory of tense conversations before they even start. Just as Christine's staff thought her office changes were shallow and materialistic, people often look at these steps as "other stuff" that aren't an immediate need in the big picture of working together better. However, it's the "other stuff" that allows for productive conflict resolution to take place.

For both people in positions of power and people on the same hierarchical level, the natural inclination to rush to solve a disagreement causes people to skip past the crucial components of establishing trust: empathy, logic, and authenticity. So we urge you not to skip through the specific and concrete action steps discussed in this chapter:

1. Collaborate on logistics

2. Plan for plenty of time

3. Clarify shared expectations

4. Establish a safe and neutral ground

The time spent on these steps can greatly reduce the time in conflict and this part of the process is essential to ensuring feelings of success in the final part—the big conversation.

CHAPTER 7

THE BIG CONVERSATION

Ready to put all of this hard work into action? Here are our hopes for you:

We hope that you've pondered the research and insights that help all of us understand the sticky nature of conflict.

We hope that you've gone through most of the exercises in chapter 5, enabling you to recognize and take responsibility for the meanings, values, feelings, and relationships that you bring to the experience of conflict.

Finally, we hope that you've done the preliminary collaborative work in chapter 6 to set up the conversation about your current, specific conflict. That work helps you establish some ground rules and regain a bit of trust, and it makes this next part much easier.

If for some reason you haven't taken the time to engage that preliminary work, we sincerely urge you to do so now. It's very tempting to turn to this chapter and dive in, to be sure. But rushing unaware into a conversation with your counterpart is virtually guaranteed to make things a whole lot worse.

If you *have* taken the time to engage that consistently challenging, often confusing, and rarely fun work, we want to share some good news: we really do think it gets easier from here.

Here are the four big reasons why.

You're Ready

Relax. For the first time in a while, perhaps your whole life, you are as prepared as you possibly can be to fully participate in an awkward, emotional, difficult discussion. Let that soak in.

This book is structured to engage all three essential parts of adult learning, and if you've made it this far, we're pretty sure you're right where you need to be. You've read the research, explanations, and examples to gain *knowledge* about conflict, both general knowledge about human conflict and specific knowledge about you as an individual engaging in it. You've

> **Truly being ready to engage in a difficult conversation about a conflict requires recognizing that you don't know what's going to happen, that you aren't in control and can't predict the path forward.**

leveraged that knowledge in each chapter to learn *skills* that you can bring into conflict, skills that you'll continue to develop here in this chapter.

But, as every early childhood educator knows, knowledge and skills aren't enough. We bet that, like us, you've sat through hours and days of professional development, learning about some new instructional strategy or technique with a group of teachers. But in the few months following the training, the skills are nowhere to be seen in classrooms, and you and your fellow teachers seem to have forgotten the understanding. Something is missing, a third essential component to true behavior change.

That something is called *mindset*. Mindset refers to the collection of attitudes and perspectives that we hold that make us value something and devalue something else, the basis of our deeply held convictions and the engine that drives the confirmation bias that sustains those convictions.

Throughout the book, we have included detailed discussions and examples to encourage you to shift your mindset about conflict. You've read about and reflected on a variety of attitudes about conflict, and you now know the key attitudes that underlie a more effective mindset. Ideally the wide range of perspectives in this book have led you to a mindset that seeks collaboration with ideas that are not your own.

We truly hope that your understanding and skills about conflict have increased markedly, as we are relying on that understanding and those skills in this chapter. And we're optimistic that your mindset has shifted sufficiently to make the steps in this chapter align with your attitudes, beliefs, and values as they morph into something more inclusive, humble, and human.

If all of that is true, you're as ready as you can be!

There's No Such Thing as "Ready"

What's more, we're optimistic that you've made the biggest mental shift of all: you know that part of being ready is accepting that you're not entirely ready. Indeed, you'll never be entirely ready. There is no such thing.

After all, if you were entirely ready to address a conflict, that might well mean that you're all set to present your solution to your counterpart, to fix what needs fixing, and to expect them to express their deep gratitude. Remember Chris's thoroughly planned parent meeting from chapter 2 that was an unmitigated disaster? He wasn't truly ready at all. Instead, he had created a false sort of readiness, one that was intended to reassure himself, not to engage conflict effectively.

Truly being ready to engage in a difficult conversation about a conflict requires recognizing that you don't know what's going to happen, that you aren't in control and can't predict the path forward. Chris forgot a central rule of all conflict resolution: difficult conversations can only be effective if they are genuinely collaborative. As a result, it's impossible to predict most of what will happen.

There is one thing you can predict, however: a successful conflict discussion requires learning. You don't know what you don't know yet, but when engaging in conflict productively, you can be sure that you'll learn something.

The big conversation ahead isn't really one moment in time. It's much bigger than that.

So if you don't feel entirely ready, you're probably ready—even if your stomach aches a bit. Accepting your ignorance and lack of control is likely to make you feel a bit panicky at times. That's because you're human; you want to know what you're getting yourself into before it starts. So if your mindset has shifted a bit and you're able to accept a lack of readiness and the slightly shaky nerves that come with it, you're set to go.

The Big Conversation Is Really, Really Big

The big conversation ahead isn't really one moment in time. It's much bigger than that. There is no question that approaching this difficult conversation is its own thing, and this chapter includes very concrete suggestions for how to engage the steps and strategies you'll need during the conversation. That said, let's face it: you're almost certainly going to have a lot more conversations with your counterpart after this one, and unless you're both outstanding practitioners of the silent treatment, you're probably having a few here and there even now. All of 'em added together? That's actually the big conversation.

This mindset is so critical for the same reason that the big conversation is really, really big. Both are not about what you do. Rather, both are about how you are. Your mindset shift will change the way you perceive things, people, situations; by definition it will change what you recognize and value. The big conversation is the same: by engaging it with effective understanding, skills, and attitudes, you'll be in the big conversation with your counterpart and many others because that will be just how you are.

Indeed, you might just decide that the really, really big conversation has another name: life.

These sorts of shifts don't happen overnight, and they don't happen by reading a book! Rather, you change the way you are in the really, really big conversation by having specific big conversations like the one you'll have soon with your counterpart. Some conversations will be more effective than others, and each of them will give you plentiful opportunities to learn more. But you don't have to be perfect—indeed, you can't be perfect.

So we urge you to engage each of the big conversations as if they're part of the really, really big conversation. Each conversation is important, but it's not everything. It's just another step along the path—a path that is pretty fascinating to us, one that keeps us learning. And knowing that each difficult encounter is merely another step forward as we find our way through conflict makes everything a whole lot calmer and easier.

We're hopeful that you are starting to feel the same way—it means you're in a position to lead.

The Opportunity of Leadership

The fourth reason that things get easier moving forward involves taking on a position of leadership in the difficult conversation itself. We urge you to lead not because it's a morally superior position (it is not, trust us) or an effective strategy (it is, trust us). Rather, in this moment, assuming a position of leadership will almost certainly make the entire affair easier for everyone involved, including you.

On more than one occasion, both Chris and Christine have had to engage in difficult conversations in which we each had to take on a leadership role whether we wanted to or not. Often these situations go surprisingly well, even if the conflicts themselves were not entirely resolved. We were as ready as we could be; we knew that our understanding, skills, and mindset were in the right place; we knew that this was part of a really, really big conversation, not just one chat.

Finally, we took a position of leadership in the discussions, setting the collaborative terms and the compassionate tone, even as we engaged in the conflict with the folks involved.

Here's Chris's story.

Dating back years, one of the preschool rooms in our school experienced problem after problem, transition after transition. In the last few weeks, a series of incidents caused several parents to confront our family engagement staff and say that they wanted out. I had been working hard to address the situation in a variety of ways, but the mess was coming to a head faster than I had anticipated.

One afternoon, the most frustrated parent arrived to pick up her child. I have a close relationship with her daughter, and I knew that she and her mom were both struggling with the classroom issues. When I looked up from my desk, I realized that she had brought the child's grandmother—a sign that things had reached an even higher level of concern. Both mom and grandma were visibly angry.

For a brief moment at first, I wanted to shut my glass door and hide behind my computer monitor. It had been a long day, and I was exhausted. But then I realized, "I may not feel ready, but I know what to do." And I walked out to talk to both of them directly.

I started the conversation by saying that I knew that they had serious concerns and by asking them what they were. They were sitting, so I kneeled down, made eye contact, and listened. As they expressed their anger and frustration, I nodded and repeated back what they said, adding sentences like "That makes a lot of sense" and "I'm seeing the same things."

After a few minutes of listening to and validating their concerns, I said a few true statements. I told them that I realized the severity of the issues and was working hard on the problem. I admitted that the agency procedures we have in place often make things move more slowly than we'd like. I told them that, though there were certain issues I had to keep confidential, I would keep them fully informed about what was happening, and that my door was open.

Finally, I thanked them for sharing their anger and frustration. "I know how hard it is to bring up a conflict with the people who care for the most important person in your life," I said. "And I'm truly grateful that you did."

The mom thanked me; the grandma . . . not so much. I hadn't solved the problem; indeed, I hadn't taken any administrative action at all. I just took the lead, validated their feelings, and assured them that our relationship was real and appreciated, and would continue.

When I saw mom the next day, she smiled and we had a brief chat, another moment in the really, really big conversation.

Here's Christine's story.

One of the most challenging parts of leading an early childhood program is supporting teaching teams. It's a lot of work getting just the right combination of teacher talent and temperament, and doing that throughout a whole building can feel like solving a complex puzzle. That alignment takes a lot of practice, intentional strategies, and sometimes multiple attempts.

At one point, I had a teaching team that struggled to get along. Teacher A didn't feel everyone was pulling their weight, teacher B felt everyone was talking behind their back, teacher C just wanted everyone to get over it, and so on. They made several attempts to work through this together, but each effort resulted in eye rolling, or yelling, or tears.

After a particularly bad interaction, they called me into a team discussion to "fix the problem." I already knew there was no magic solution to make this team (or any team) work cohesively together, particularly given the big feelings that had been growing over weeks. But

I also knew it was an opportunity to model some qualities that were central to my leadership style: expressing difficulty using neutral and child-focused language, owning my contributions, considering perspectives other than my own, and, especially, sitting in discomfort instead of rushing to "fix" a problem.

I didn't do much talking at all. Instead, I spent most of my time listening. When I did talk, I often took up someone else's position or words, restating what each person had to say and drawing connections between the teachers' perspectives. I wasn't pushing toward my solution, whatever that would have been. Instead, I wanted them to hear their own ideas and thoughts, both individual and shared, and to help them see places of agreement. Only after all of their insights and feelings were on the table did we start naming a set of imperfect potential solutions.

As you can imagine, we didn't pick a solution that day. But we did sit together, express our perspectives, name our feelings, identify our common goals and values about working for children, and consider possible ways to reconnect as a team. We didn't solve the problem, but we left with a calm sense of collaboration that hadn't existed before. We had taken a step forward, learning together how to function differently as a team.

There are a lot of consistent details from previous chapters woven through these two stories. Both of us decided we need to turn toward and step into the conflict instead of turning away from it; both of us sought to learn by engaging the perspective of others with respect. Chris was Chris and Christine was Christine, yet both of us were as comfortable as could be expected given our imperfections, nervousness, and the mess we were in.

But we also demonstrated leadership grounded in the skills, understanding, and mindset we've charted in this book. We took the first step in a collaborative discussion, initiating it and staying engaged. We knew we didn't have it all figured out and admitted that. What we did in the conversations was important, but how we did those things was more important. And we took the lead by using the strategies we explain in this chapter, strategies that are so simple to learn and use that it's easy to misperceive their incredible power.

Taking the lead in conflict almost always makes things easier for that reason: simple steps are the most powerful. So let's get started with the difficult encounter itself.

Conversation Step 1: Start with What Happened

As Robin and Pat demonstrate in chapter 4, every difficult conversation is a three-in-one. The conversation will activate feelings with which we're familiar: frustration, disappointment, anger, shame, you name it. In addition, the conversation and the feelings are difficult because, in some way or another, our identity is at stake.

It may be tempting to start your discussion by asking about feelings and identity, getting to the meat of the problem right away. But when you're in a conflict with someone, you're very unlikely to want to talk openly and honestly about complex feelings and a threatened sense of identity. After all, trust is weak or entirely missing, and that means your relationship lacks the security and intimacy that such open, honest talk requires.

The discussion on brain states reminds us that when you jump into difficult feelings and identity concerns, you risk moving from your executive state into an emotional state—or worse. The goal of every difficult conversation should be to learn, and that means finding a way to start the conversation in a manner that feels familiar, reasonable, and collaborative.

Early childhood educators have been trained in a very specific skill that provides us with benefits in conflict.

Thankfully, early childhood educators have been trained in a very specific skill that provides us with benefits in conflict, the skill of child observation. Every day, early childhood educators must observe children in their activities, noting where they are developmentally, how they respond to changes and challenges, and what their strengths and areas of growth are.

In doing so, we need to keep our biases, preferences, and judgments at bay. When Chris teaches observation in his child development classes, he stresses that every documented observation should SOAR: it should be specific, objective, accurate, and responsible. You may use a different acronym, but all early childhood educators know the importance of high-quality observation and assessment documentation.

But it takes practice. For example, a student just starting out in our field might write the following as an anecdotal record:

> Precious was so frustrated because she didn't get a turn with the dolls. She made such a fuss that she couldn't sit still at group time. The teacher must like her a bunch, because she put up with a lot of bad behavior. But finally Precious sat still and listened to the story. That child's mother needs a talking-to!

This anecdote surely doesn't soar! Let us count the ways:

It is not *specific*: "couldn't sit still"; "put up with a lot of bad behavior."

It is not *objective*: "bad behavior"; "couldn't sit still"; "mother needs a talking-to!"

It is not *responsible*: "teacher must like her a bunch"; "mother needs a talking-to!"

And, finally, given all of those problems, one has to wonder about exactly how *accurate* the documentation is, right? After all, what do some of these terms even mean?

Compare that description to the very different one below, one that might have been written by a teacher who knows how to make observational documentation soar:

> Precious waited for another child to finish using a doll that she said she wanted, standing next to the child and fidgeting with her hands. Then the teacher told the class to transition to the large rug for group time. When she did, Precious looked around the room and said, "But I didn't get a turn!" Tearing up, she stood by the pretend play area and refused to leave, even when a teacher asked her to do so.
>
> After a couple of minutes, with some guidance, Precious walked over to and sat down at her spot on the rug, but she kept looking over at the pretend play area where the dolls were, and at times stood to walk over to that area. The teacher sat next to her, reassuring her that she would have a turn after the book reading, and each time Precious sat down and crossed her arms with a frown on her face. After two or three attempts to leave, she turned her attention to the other teacher reading the book.

Do you see how much easier it is to picture what happened in this anecdote? It's specific, providing vivid details that help you see the moment as it unfolds. It is also objective: we can imagine nearly any person witnessing the situation writing the same account consistently. Finally, it's responsible: there's no blame or judgment to be found. It's just a kid being a kid.

Soaring observations are essential for adult conflict too, and if they are missing things get messy fast. Remember Robin and Pat? Jump back to chapter 4 if you'd like two versions of what happened that really, really don't soar! As a comparison, here's what a third, uninvolved observer might have recorded about Robin and Pat to create specific, objective, accurate, and responsible documentation.

> Pat and Robin work together. Pat grew up in this community and Robin did not. During staff discussions, when Robin speaks, Pat often leans back in the chair and looks silently at the ceiling. When Pat speaks, Robin often turns to colleagues and discusses the topic with them.
>
> Robin devotes a lot of time and effort to building relationships with families in this community. Pat often steps into conversations Robin is having with families, using words about helping. When Pat does so, Robin often stops interacting with the families, stepping back from the discussion.
>
> Robin interacts regularly with the director, spending time in their office and talking in the hallway. Pat has never gone into the director's office or had an informal chat with them. The director asked Pat how things were going between the two of them. Pat smiled and said, "Great!" as Robin watched.
>
> Pat initiated a conversation with a mother and infant concerning some governmental forms the mother had to fill out. Robin walked up and offered to help both Pat and the mother, then Pat walked away from the discussion.

Both Robin and Pat should be able to agree completely that this description depicts what happened. That's because the description soars. And that's the key to getting what happened right.

To use your soaring observation skills with your counterpart, start the conversation by describing what you observed. Even with very different versions of the feelings you bring as individuals to this conflict, you need to agree on the basic details of the situation if you're going to find your way through the conflict. Use specifics, because general categories make things messy. Be objective, so that everyone can agree on what happened. Be accurate, because inaccuracy smacks of judgment and eradicates trust. Lastly, be responsible: assuming intent, playing gotcha, and extrapolating with words like "always" and "never" are irresponsible and destructive.

The specific, objective, accurate, and responsible information provides the foundation for the trickier parts that come next. We have just the tool to make the trickier parts work: looping.

Conversation Step 2: Loop Your Way Through the Conflict

There are very few magic wands in our world, and fewer still in the world of conflict. But we firmly believe that the skill of looping is one of them, a skill that is vital to situations like the ones above and virtually every other conflict we've come across. In this section, we show you why this magic wand is the best tool in your tool kit.

Not only does looping benefit you as an easy way to start the big conversation, it benefits your counterpart too. By asking your counterpart to tell their story, you're eliciting the exact thing that they fear you want to ignore, debate, or erase. And because it initiates your collaborative effort to find your way through conflict, looping benefits both the conflict's resolution and the relationship that will sustain that resolution.

Sounds pretty great, doesn't it? Let's break it into its three parts: inquire, restate, and acknowledge.

Inquire

Something quite wonderful happens when someone asks, "How are you?" and means it. A social pleasantry that is usually empty becomes a gesture of connection. Suddenly, someone in the world cares enough to pause and include a moment of our life into their own.

For most people, "How are you?" is a throwaway comment, something you say like "Good morning!" or "Hi!" It's less a question than a declaration that you're being polite to another person.

But in conflict we need to learn to ask questions like "How are you?" for real. Leading with genuine inquiry initiates the path through which the conversation can unfold.

Inquiry thus includes two complementary components: the question and the silent listening after the question.

By asking questions because you want to know the answer, not because you want to provide your own response, you reset the relationship with your counterpart. Of course, if you are seeking connection to that person, the word *counterpart* starts to feel too clinical and detached. So, starting here, we are going to retire the word *counterpart*, replacing it with something better suited for finding your way through conflict together. This person is now your *collaborator*.

The best inquiry starts by recapitulating what happened in the situation that has caused the conflict. To lead, you want to start not with your own version but with the one told from your collaborator's perspective. Conveniently, there's a straightforward request to use: "So, from your perspective, tell me what happened."

It's that simple. All you have to do is look your collaborator in the eye, pause, and ask what happened. That's how you lead. It happens so rarely in our lives, and its rarity gives it remarkable power as an act of connection and respect.

Once you make that request, you have to do a second thing that's rare in the human world. You need to shut up. Nod. Maintain eye contact. Use your ears. Attend.

You need to actively listen.

We joke about this a lot in our own relationship, because we've had to learn how to do a better job of actively listening to each other over the years. For the most part, that's been because we tend to think alike, want to finish each other's sentences, shout out "You said it!" and so on. As a result of that connection, both of us have had to work on our own listening skills.

Truth be told . . . one of us has had to work on those skills more than the other. Chris tends to think by talking, a perfectly acceptable personality trait in many situations—but not in conflict. Many, many times, Chris has caught Christine smiling and nodding with a bit of self-amused glee, the indication that, a few moments before, he jumped in to affirm, add on, and otherwise enthusiastically give a verbal high five. They were all positive interjections, but that didn't erase the fact that Chris, a man, felt authorized to interrupt Christine, a woman.

Support is great, don't get us wrong! But support that squelches another person's story isn't supportive in conflict, particularly if the person is jumping in to explain the point he is interrupting. It's silencing—friendly, affable silencing. And if it's a man mansplaining a woman's ideas back to her? That's probably part of the problem.

So Chris has learned, over the years, to follow his inquiries—of Christine and everyone else—with a very specific gesture: he puts his hand over his mouth. Given that Chris knows he's going to Chris it, he's developed a simple tool to make sure that he shuts up and stays shut up, using his hand to do what his brain sometimes cannot.

Inquiry thus includes two complementary components: the question and the silent listening after the question. Both work in tandem; neither work alone. You need to do the two-fold inquiry part well, or else the next two parts of looping are impossible.

Restate

Over the years, we've fiddled with the word to describe this step. At one point we used the word *paraphrase*, which is defined as repeating what someone else has said using different words. The problems started there: in choosing different words, you get yourself into trouble. Suddenly, a word you thought was equivalent is a bone of contention; instead of capturing the essence of someone's recollection, your summary leaves out the most important part.

So part two of looping is to *restate* what someone has said. In conflict, you want to demonstrate that you've listened. You want your collaborator to hear their views and experiences coming out of your mouth. And that means restating the answer, using the same words and phrases that your collaborator used. It's a less interpretive action than paraphrasing or summarizing, which in a situation lacking trust is an important characteristic.

In some ways, restating is very straightforward. After your collaborator has told you what happened from their perspective, you demonstrate that you were listening to and valuing their words by sharing them back. Simple enough . . . if you're careful. Focus on restating their objective description of their perspective. Of course, when emotions run high, defensive and sometimes offensive language can slip in, so you should only restate the neutral components.

Once again, remember that how you do something is more important than the thing itself. Yes, restating someone's words can be an affirming indication that you care about and respect what they've shared. But if you do so while rolling your eyes and robotically repeating the exact same sentences, you're going to make things worse, not better.

Here's where mindset is everything. When you restate what your collaborator has said, you need to do so out of full respect that their perspective is legitimate, that what happened to them is just as important as what happened to you. You need to want to learn what that was like.

Thankfully, the third part of looping functions not only to move the conversation forward but to make sure that your mindset is in tune with your priority to move through the conflict. This last part is your insurance policy that you are looping for real.

Acknowledge

Acknowledgment isn't agreement.

Read that again.

This sentence is so important that we encourage you to write it on a sticky note and put it on your computer monitor. You could even consider a tattoo—we think it's that important. Before we dive into why it's so crucial, let's walk through the skill itself.

> Declaring the legitimacy of someone else's perspective does not diminish the legitimacy of your own. Rather, your perspective will have legitimacy in your collaborator's eyes to the extent that theirs has legitimacy in your own.

Acknowledgment is the declaration of the legitimacy of your collaborator's position. As part of looping, acknowledgment serves to validate your sincerity and trustworthiness. After all, if you don't acknowledge what you just restated, you're just playing some insincere game with your collaborator. It's in both your and your collaborator's interest for you to validate and legitimate the words that came out of, first, their mouth and, second, your own.

How you do this couldn't be simpler. To acknowledge what someone has said (and you've restated) requires saying one of a small number of sentences and meaning it fully. "That makes sense." "I really understand." "That seems completely reasonable." "Of course." You make eye contact. You nod.

Easy peasy, right? Careful . . . maybe not so much.

When you read those sentences, thinking about your collaborator, did you find yourself adding phrases to them? "That makes sense—from your perspective." "I really understand—that you don't understand." "That seems completely reasonable—if you don't have all the facts!" "Of course—of course you'd think that, you moron!"

If those addendums keep popping into your head, that means your mindset needs a quick tune-up. Finding your way through conflict requires you to engage your collaborator's perspective as valid, as legitimate. Put differently, it's time to stop thinking your collaborator is a convenient fiction that you use to confirm your bias, stay stuck, and defend your position in a conflict. It's time to fully recognize the humanity of the other person.

Acknowledgment both requires and expands that recognition. That's why all collaborative progress through conflict requires acknowledgment as the foundation for every step. The best way to give your mindset a tune-up is to remind yourself of the sentiment that started the section.

Acknowledgment isn't agreement. To make acknowledgment work, you need to keep Peter Elbow's insight, shared in chapter 5, close at hand: you are always right, and you are always wrong.

What does that mean for you in your big conversation? We encourage you to remind yourself, over and over, that declaring the legitimacy of someone else's perspective does not diminish the legitimacy of your own. Rather, your perspective will have legitimacy in your collaborator's eyes to the extent that theirs has legitimacy in your own. In the learning conversation that moves you through conflict, both people's perspectives are in dialogue, informing and expanding each other.

So practice acknowledgment if you fear your defenses and judgment will make it difficult. Thankfully, there are lots of opportunities to do so. Customer service complaints, children who whine about household chores: the world will generously provide you with opportunities to assert acknowledgment without agreement. It's a useful skill!

Conversation Step 3: Relate Alternative Perspectives

Generating respect for your collaborator's perspective is the foundation for the next step, in which you ask that person to expand your shared sphere of acknowledgment. It requires a large dose of the intellectual humility discussed in chapter 3—that sense that your take on things is limited and that it's important to approach any explanation in a curious, humble manner.

At this point, you've already led the way to a preliminary sense of intellectual humility thanks to your inquiry about and acknowledgment of your collaborator's version of things. We hope that they have extended you the same opportunity, but even if they haven't, you can take the next step by exploring what other perspectives might be floating around.

Our work as early childhood educators is relentlessly social. We typically work in teams, and we interact daily with the parents and guardians we serve. Most of us work in programs or centers with administrators in and out of our rooms, plus directors, coaches, and education coordinators who interact with us throughout the day. Most importantly, we interact hundreds of times each day with the children in our care.

All of these relationships and interactions form a network through which our conflicts travel, whether we like it or not. That means that, even in the most thorough discussions with another person, the two perspectives you've shared between each other are but a fraction of the perspectives you need to consider.

Of course, you can't know everything about the perspectives other than the ones the two of you share, but you can start by asking questions about who else is impacted by your big conversation. Then, for each impacted person, speculate together about what perspective they might have.

Robin and Pat can help you with this. How might another colleague perceive the conflict Robin and Pat are in—and, as a result, how might that person perceive Robin or Pat? What would it be like to be one of the parents involved, someone who, when seeking assistance, instead consistently finds themselves in the midst of a mysterious tussle? Most importantly, what must it be like to be the small child with that parent?

Each of these questions is worth a few minutes of curious, collaborative exploration. The goal here is not to settle on an interpretation; your intellectual humility should keep that impulse in check. Rather, your goal is to learn. It's time to expand your understanding of the conflict, to move past your perspectives and the intentions that motivate them to include a consideration of the impact your actions, individual and shared, have had.

Which brings us to the final piece of this big conversation.

Conversation Step 4: Consider Contributions (and Avoid Blame)

In a perfect world, you would be here at the outset. "Let's sit down, explore how we created this mess, and make sure it doesn't happen again." As human beings, however, you and your collaborator need to build some understanding, trust, and skill before you can arrive at this place.

Most importantly, you need to jettison blame. Almost certainly, at the start of this process, you were pretty committed to blaming your counterpart. If you're like us, blame was the primary motivation for engaging the conflict in the first place. Hopefully, your impulse to blame has weakened as you've learned to see its limitations. Blame blinds you to other contributions impacting the conflict—and there are always other contributions.

Early childhood educators are impacted by a cluster of consistently overlooked contributions related to how the work and the people in early childhood education are astoundingly undervalued. Every bit of research about child development, academic achievement, and lifelong learning makes it clear that teaching the youngest children is the most important work on the planet. And yet early childhood educators struggle for resources, recognition, and respect.

We believe that many of the conflicts among early childhood educators are deeply impacted by the systemic inequities built into early childhood education in the United States. Poor wages mean that we earn far less than we deserve. Lack of adequate health care and other benefits make our trying jobs more stressful and unhealthy. Insufficient social service networks provide few options for children and families impacted by abuse, neglect, food insecurity, and other challenges, leaving us to support the traumatized survivors with few tools.

Finally, broad, deep-seated structural inequities are embedded in our field. Caring for young children is traditionally and practically a women's profession, and gendered misperceptions demean the crucial work we do every day as "mere babysitting." That work is performed largely by women whose identities reflect the communities they serve, and structural racism demeans the crucial work of those Black, Latinx, and indigenous women, as well as that of other women of color.

Given that those relentless inequities structure our work, it stands to reason that we struggle with conflict and consistently want to acknowledge those inequities in our conflicts as true contributions, particularly when they don't seem apparent at first. Here are two examples to help illustrate this.

Very often in his program, Chris and his team run into conflicts when talking to a family that can't sort out a problem with their DHS subsidy. At first glance, it can appear that the family has missed appointment after appointment due to their carelessness, but that blame is an inadequate, inappropriate misunderstanding.

The list of issues contributing to this category of conflict is very long: insufficient funding for hiring, training, and retaining DHS case workers; English-only materials; inadequate hours of operation for office hours; and a poor public transit system that doesn't reach our families' neighborhoods. By the time we approach a family to discuss a lapsed subsidy problem, it's likely that they've already had a dozen frustrating experiences.

Here's an even more common example.

Christine and Chris each devote many hours coaching teachers who struggle with a child who's having complex behavior issues. It's easy to see that conflict between teacher and child in isolation, but there is a similarly long list of additional contributions fueling that conflict.

Few early childhood education preparation programs offer extensive coursework and practicum training in working with complex behavioral issues. Despite its research-based approach, trauma-responsive care is poorly embedded in the curricula, professional development, and coaching systems most programs use. Meanwhile, parents struggling with these same behaviors at home have few support services to access—and in most school districts their child faces a severely diminished set of supports when they transition out of most early childhood education programs.

Our society's structural inequities contribute to nearly all conflicts in our field, especially conflicts in which those inequities seemingly aren't in play. In our experiences, a frank consideration of those contributions, while sobering, is a useful part of learning about the true extent of the situation we are seeking to address.

In addition, a frank consideration of structural factors gives you and your collaborator the opportunity to express your good faith attempts to address them, even in the midst of the conflict. You're in this imperfect world together, and within that world you're doing the best you can. And, despite your intentions, you've contributed to the conflict as well.

In the introduction, we state that conflict is nearly always reciprocal. In nearly every conflict you're in, you have contributed.

Once again, this recognition presents you with an opportunity to take the lead. We have found that, while we are acknowledging someone else's perspective when looping, we add other sentences

> Our society's structural inequities contribute to nearly all conflicts in our field, especially conflicts in which those inequities seemingly aren't in play.

we hadn't expected we would add, sentences like "I can see how my doing that would be frustrating," "Oh, that's how you perceived my action!" and "Wow, I didn't realize I came off like that." These sentences and others like them are acknowledgments of contributions we've made to the conflict, despite our good intentions and usually without being aware of the impact.

Acknowledging your contributions is remarkably powerful—if you acknowledge them in the proper spirit. As always, it's not just what you do; it's also how you do it. A humble recognition of your complicity works; a sarcastic "So *I'm* the one who's at fault here!" does not. And retaining your own story is essential: after all, if conflict is nearly always reciprocal, your collaborator contributed too.

If you're truly in a collaborative dialogue about contributions, it's likely that a lot of other insights are revealing themselves to you as well. You may want to share some of them; for example, this is a good time to explain why you have strong feelings of disrespect when someone unintentionally does or says a particular thing. Meanwhile, you may be noting other insights that are a bit too risky to share with your collaborator. Those insights are absolutely critical: make a mental or written note of them and commit to returning to them as you move forward, because this conflict isn't going away without you confronting them on your own or with a trusted colleague.

Every contribution you identify, in dialogue or solitude, is an opportunity to learn more about conflict. They'll help you find your way through this conflict with greater skill, but until you situate those insights within the big conversation that is life, you'll keep bumping into them in each succeeding conflict. Your insights are the history you had chosen to forget, but in finding your way through conflict, you are finding your way through yourself!

Continuing the Big Conversation

Careful listening. Acknowledging each other's story. Exploring additional perspectives and contributions.

What we've charted in this chapter are strategies that we've found are the key to finding your way through conflict. We don't know any way through conflict without them; every other strategy that works incorporates these in some way or another.

But this chapter is about the big conversation; it's about how you do what you do. Listening, acknowledgment, exploration of perspectives and contributions: these are ways of doing the work of early childhood education, and even of being in the world in general. And they all come from our deepest knowledge and training about child development.

At every stage of development, children need adults to listen to them. Babies babbling; twos showing you their ball or shoe or finger; preschoolers demanding "Why?"; kindergarteners explaining dinosaur taxonomy: all children need caring, attentive adults who listen to them, who acknowledge their story and perspective. It's a human need, one that we believe all adults share as well, and certainly all adults who found their way into this remarkable profession.

Every stage of development is, well, a stage of development. Like the children we serve, we have endless opportunities to learn, and our brains retain the ability to shift and grow throughout adulthood. Whether we call it lifelong learning, growth mindset, or simple, humble curiosity, approaching each experience as an opportunity to learn and grow is, we feel, a professional and personal imperative.

To recap, here are your action steps for the big conversation:

1. Start with what happened

2. Loop your way through conflict

3. Relate alternative perspectives

4. Consider contributions (and avoid blame)

This is an ongoing process of engagement. We will always be finding our way through conflict. We will never reach the end.

But you want to get to the conclusion, don't you? Of course you do!

CHAPTER 8

WE NEVER STOP LEARNING ABOUT CONFLICT

You have no doubt realized that we didn't actually provide ways to solve your problem. Each time we have facilitated this content as a workshop, someone has asked us, "Okay, fine, but what is the solution?" We'd love to live in a world that has a simple answer to that question, once and for all!

So . . . we have to make a confession. This conclusion won't exactly conclude anything. That's not to say that we won't make a few concluding remarks. We do have some takeaways to share, some last thoughts that we think you'll find valuable. Perhaps unfortunately (but predictably), we have no final, definitive answer to all the problems. We aren't going to share some cure-all strategies that will permanently inoculate you from conflict. By now we hope you know that such things don't exist.

There are no final steps that will solve your current conflict at hand. We've learned the hard way that predicting such steps is a dangerous game. There are no quick fixes.

This is one of the key insights from *Systems Thinking for Social Change* by David Peter Stroh. In his essential book, Stroh articulates a research-based approach to solving complex problems, avoiding unintended consequences, and achieving lasting results. You are already familiar with several of his insights, such as resisting blame and recognizing that "we unwittingly create our own problems and have significant control or influence in solving them through changing our own actions" (Stroh 2015, 15). In many ways, that quotation is the beating heart of the book you're holding now.

Stroh's application of systems thinking to social change has transformed our own thinking about conflict. He urges us to tell systems stories, in which we construct a depiction of a situation from multiple perspectives, acknowledging the reality of each. Like finding your way through conflict, this work is relentlessly collaborative; we need each other to solve problems. We simply can't do it alone, and a book won't change that fact.

Stroh's distinction between conventional thinking and systems thinking reveals the problem with definitive conclusions. Because human beings are thoroughly, endlessly dynamic, the systems that we build and implement are dynamic as well. It's all change, flux, development; you can't pin life down.

However, humans want our problems to sit still. We want to isolate them so that those problems can be fixed. This is the core of Stroh's understanding of the central error of conventional thinking: we wrongly believe that "in order to optimize the whole, we must optimize the parts" (2015, 15). In the world of conflict, conventional thinking works in the same way: to solve problems in our interactions, people desperately seek discrete elements that should be fixed or removed or replaced.

> The focus of our approach is developing skills and comfort being *in* conflict situations.

We, along with Stroh, have learned that such conventional thinking is part of the problem itself. The quick fixes and to-do lists get us further stuck in conflict. They blind us to the ways that conflict works, its nuances and complexities, and they lead to perpetuating the causes that generate conflicts in the first place.

Instead, we suggest that you embrace a systems perspective that recognizes that, as Stroh puts it, "in order to optimize the whole, we must improve the relationships among the parts" (2015, 15). Stroh has used this insight to address massive social problems that are the focus of some of the world's most important organizations, including the Centers for Disease Control and the World Bank. We're convinced that it's just as powerful an insight for us as early childhood educators. (And we're convinced that interpersonal conflict is just as important as any other social problem.)

So, like Stroh, we urge you to resist that nagging quick-fix urge. To find your way through conflict, you have to improve the relationships among the contributors to the conflict. Some relationships are structural; some are outside of your control. But we think Stroh is correct when he says that everyone can "have significant control or influence [by] changing our own actions." You and the other person can have far more impact than you think by changing your own actions within your relationship. Only by accepting a relationship-forward mindset will you be able to find your way through conflict.

As we explained in the introduction, the focus of our approach is developing skills and comfort being *in* conflict situations. We want you to find your way through conflict in both senses of the word *through*. Yes, we want you to make your way into and out of any given conflict, to pass through it. But we also want you to use conflict to find your way forward, for conflict itself to be the means, the path through.

Finally, all that you've learned on the path so far is absolutely essential to developing a skillful response in conflict. Indeed, the skills, understanding, and mindset you've developed are exactly what you need.

The Tools in Your New Tool Kit

When conflict comes your way, you'll see it for what it is, an essential form of perspective-taking. Your understanding of conflict now includes recognition that everyone has slightly different definitions of conflict, and you see the value of exploring the inevitably different perspectives of others.

You know how to *shift from reaction to response* by reflecting on your initial reaction and forming a personal response that recognizes your contributions in conflict situations. And you know that *you need to become very familiar with who you are in conflict.* That's the person who shows up every time—whether you like the way "you" are showing up or not.

You now have the *attitudes* to learn from the sticky parts of conflict: nonjudgmental reflection, humble curiosity, and self-effacing humor. You know to keep them in mind all while also keeping an eye on *your brain state*.

You are prepared for *the big conversation* with the tools to create a *firm personal foundation* for the work ahead, checking your goals, supports, and investments and committing to your story.

The tools to *build and rebuild trust* with your collaborator will allow you to take good care of the critical logistical components of the conversation ahead. Finally, you are prepared to *lead the way through conflict* in the discussion with your collaborator, *looping* extensively and bringing in lots of *other perspectives*.

These tools are the skills, understanding, and mindset that you need to work with the other person as you establish a response to your shared situation. But even more than before, the key to finding your way through conflict at this stage involves true collaboration. So before you dive into that process, you need to consider one final, very important question.

Choosing the Right Approach

This book is primarily focused on a specific approach to conflict: direct engagement with a collaborator. Of course, at this point in your situation, we are hoping that you've found another person willing to work with you to determine your next move together. But we realize that's not always the case. So before you jump into that approach, you need to determine whether it's the right one for this situation.

In her important book, *HBR Guide to Dealing with Conflict, Harvard Business Review* editor Amy Gallo identifies four options for dealing with conflict:

Do nothing.

Address indirectly.

Address directly.

Exit the relationship (Gallo 2017).

We've chosen to focus solely on addressing the conflict directly because early childhood educators routinely avoid that option. We wrote this book to help you develop skill and composure in the moment of conflict, if for no other reason than to develop corresponding conflict resolution skills with young children.

But directly addressing conflict is not always the best approach, even in early childhood education programs. There are certainly circumstances in which one of the other options Gallo describes is the right fit for the situation, and those options are important to keep in mind.

For example, sometimes a conflict relates to a temporary concern or brief challenge. In those situations, perhaps doing nothing but waiting it out is the right move. Similarly, if you do not feel that you can engage productively with a disrespectful colleague but can limit your interactions with them, addressing the problem indirectly with avoidance may be the way to go. Finally, if you are having conflicts that you can end by severing a personal relationship that has grown from a professional one, remember that you don't have to attend every party to which you are invited. Graceful exits, we find, have their place in our remarkably social profession.

So which approach is correct in your situation? We urge you to reflect carefully on this question. As you do, keep an eye on your anxieties, imperfections, and fears, especially if you are considering an option other than direct address. Of course, you should not subject yourself to abuse, disrespect, or other severe issues. (A colleague, supervisor, or your HR administrator can help you sort those out.) But, if you can, be courageous. Don't let your trepidation dictate your approach.

Only you can determine the right option. We're going to assume that, as it is for us, the direct approach is the right way through most of the conflicts you face—even though it might not be the most appealing one at first.

Developing a Provisional Response

All this amazing work prepares you to develop a provisional response to your conflict. Provisional responses are not steps or strategies, because they aren't a recipe. Rather, they are approaches that you can use to move your relationship with the other person forward. They are responsive to the situation at hand, and they are provisional because, by definition, "the situation at hand" is changing all the time.

Like the strategies for being in conflict, these approaches for identifying and developing a response are relentlessly collaborative. Keep incorporating the prior collaborative insights you've identified thus far, for that initial collaboration provides the foundation for all that follows.

Invite Input

The most effective way to help any group of people to get on board with a plan for moving forward is to include them in the process of coming up with ideas and choosing one together.

This approach works when solving classroom problems with children; who better to determine what to do on a field-trip rain-out or how to solve the turn-taking dilemma in the dinosaur area? This basic collaborative insight is also true when leading a team of adults. People are more likely to engage in and stay committed to a solution determined in a process in which they felt seen and heard.

So that's the principle behind this approach. Once again, you're going to take a leadership role and invite your collaborator to contribute input before you offer yours. That's not because your ideas are bad! It's because they aren't the best starting point.

Consider an instance when you have been handed a solution or forced into a prescribed outcome by someone else. Was the situation smoothly resolved and the relationship repaired? Chances are you were resistant and probably not invested, and possibly you didn't even understand the solution. Most of us would likely make a meager attempt to comply, to be sure. But did you eventually find it impossible to maintain adherence to the solution handed to you—or did you just shrug it off?

You're going for something much more effective. Given that you've already established a collaborative framework, you're going to use it to create opportunities for exploratory input, giving the other person's insights and ideas a chance to weave into your own. That input is far likelier to lead to a stable response with investment from both parties.

Here are three components of this approach, presented in no particular order but consistent with our discussion of perspective in earlier chapters. Be flexible; depending on your personality or the actual situation, some of these might be easier to explore than others.

Elicit the ideas of the other person. Make space for them, using your looping skills to draw them out. You are almost certainly going to be tempted to judge them, but the goal here is to generate ideas, not evaluate them, so keep that judgment at bay for now—even if you are certain the ideas are wrong. After all, everyone deserves to be heard, and your humble curiosity should remind you that other people always have ideas you haven't even considered yet. Finally, remember the key insight that acknowledgement is a fundamental sign of listening with respect. It is not the same as agreement. So acknowledge away!

Share your ideas clearly—and with humble curiosity. We've found that folks tend to fall into two camps. Some are convinced that their ideas aren't worth sharing or that doing so will make them vulnerable. If that's the case with you, we say: please don't worry! Sharing your ideas is a great approach *especially* if they aren't very good and make you anxious. After all, you're trying to sort through this with someone else, and showing that you are truly invested and imperfect is a smart move. You may be in the other camp, sure that your ideas are the best. That's when humble curiosity is your friend.

Seek outside input. Even if you've done a great job of collaborating up until now, chances are pretty good that the two of you are hampered by your limited vision. So consider the benefits of a third, fourth, or fifth perspective. You might invite another person into the conversation who has experience with the matter at hand, or bring in other resources like articles and books to generate ideas. Simply asking someone who knows the two of you and has seen your relationship in play can provide powerful insights.

Open-Space Brainstorming

As you gather each person's input and consider external resources, resist the urge to discount any idea, even ones that aren't currently working or could seemingly never work. We and others refer to this approach as open-space brainstorming. We want to give our collaboratively generated ideas lots of room to bump into each other, combine, compare, and grow. When we start eliminating ideas, we could unintentionally eliminate a contribution to a solution.

Here's an example from Christine's leadership in a new program.

Starting a new job in a new program, my new team and I had many opportunities to solve problems together! We used open-space brainstorming often, enabling me both to maintain respect for their experiences and to resist taking over the problem-solving process with my own previously successful strategies.

Confronted with the challenges of relationship-building and team development in our changing program, a working group of teachers and I sat down to brainstorm. With great energy, one person said, "I know! Let's all fifty of us fly down to Florida for a vacation together!"

Like most early childhood educators, I am not in command of a six-figure staff holiday budget. So I laughed, playfully rolled my eyes, and said, "Well, that's never going to happen." Trying to get back to the work at hand—or, rather, the work that I *thought* we should be doing in that moment—I replaced that obviously un-fundable idea with a free one of my own: "I was thinking more along the lines of icebreakers at the beginning of staff meetings."

One of the people on my team who was forming a new relationship with me laughed and then said, "Remember, we don't discount ideas—not even you can." The comment stopped me in my tracks.

I was thrilled that she made that comment for many reasons. It was a great moment for my relationship with the team. I knew they trusted that I live my expectations as a leader and I genuinely want to be called out. That made me so happy!

But it was great for another reason directly related to the problem at hand. When she disrupted my dismissal of the Florida junket, she created the space for a solution no one had ever considered. Up to that point, all teachers had been going to local and out-of-state professional learning events individually. But the idea of a Florida team trip got people talking about the benefits of traveling with colleagues. After a while, we agreed that sending teachers in pairs and teams to professional events was a great idea to start implementing—so we did!

A few months later, when we debriefed on this new approach, we realized it had lots of benefits we had never considered. For example, we learned that traveling together enabled teachers to hear the same ideas at the same time and then brainstorm implementation together, sharing equal contributions because they had equal access to the new information. Traveling and being out of town together also created meaningful connections and bonding that I couldn't create through icebreakers.

That is to say: we saw real benefits from an approach that we would've missed out on altogether if we had tossed out the Florida team vacation idea.

It takes practice to get comfortable with this approach. So here are a few reminders:

Simply pause and make space for ideas that you hadn't previously considered. Resist the physical urge to discount an idea. Pause, breathe, and let it exist in a pool of possibilities.

Document relentlessly. Seeing your idea in writing helps to validate it; seeing another's idea in writing enters your brain in different ways than hearing it spoken.

Remember there is more than one way to solve a problem. Even if you have been in this situation before and you know of a solution that worked in the past, this instance might require a different outcome.

Trust each other to be problem-solvers. No one knows exactly how conflicts are going to work out, but you can always front trust and show up as your best self. You can do this. The other person can too.

Choose a Provisional Response Together

Here we are, nearly at the end of the book, and you're finally at the moment of determining the response to the conflict! You've got a stack of potential responses collected in collaboration with the other person, and now it's time to make some decisions. Here are a few recommendations to keep in mind:

Choose one to start. You don't necessarily have to get it right on the first try, but you need a starting place. And you'll learn more by making one tweak instead of throwing several responses together that make insights harder to spy later on.

Consider an idea that's not yours first. This could be a growth opportunity for you to try something new or unfamiliar. Doing so is especially important if you are in a leadership role, because you demonstrate the value of your team by holding up their responses as priorities.

Anticipate needed adjustments, now or later. The response will unfold over time, so consider whether you should make a few tweaks, either at the outset or midway through implementation.

Make sure each person is on board. Take the time to check in and gauge each person's response and consent to try the idea proposed. Does everyone understand what is being agreed upon? Does everyone understand their role in the solution? Now is the time to ask.

Make Mistakes

Now prepare for imperfection. We rarely see folks land on the right response straightaway, and even if the idea is sound, execution is likely to be rocky at times.

So please remember that, like all aspects of conflict, implementing your response should be a learning process. You aren't always going to get it right, and you could get it really, really wrong! Your response may not work initially, and it may meet the needs of only some of those involved. That's not a sign of failure if you are approaching this response as an opportunity to learn.

> Let's face it: conflicts are rarely over after the first conversation or attempt at resolution.

When it happens, take a step back. Consider what worked in your process, what factors you may have overlooked, and what other ideas you can try. Your positive, collaborative, humble attitude is key. Allow yourself and others to fall down, dust off your knees, and get back up again. Be gentle with each other in the learning process.

And remember Stroh's vital insight: simply by trying and failing together, you and your collaborator are improving the relationship you share. What you do is truly less important than how you do it.

Follow Up

Remember, we're ultimately focused on the really, really big conversation we call life, and not the one-time, fix-it conversation that produces a provisional response. Let's face it: conflicts are rarely over after the first conversation or attempt at resolution. Even if it seems everything worked out, one additional conversation in which you follow up with each other and reflect is vital. After all, what a great opportunity to celebrate a rare interpersonal success!

So part of your conversation about your provisional response should include a decision about when and how to follow up. Remember to consider who needs to be involved, an appropriate time, and an appropriate space for having this discussion.

In the follow-up conversation, each person should have a chance to express their perspective on both the process and the response thus far. Take lots of time to identify things that have worked and to consider any possible adjustments that could make the outcome and situation even more successful. Remember that this is a learning opportunity, so explore progress being made and, more importantly, what isn't working.

Doing this follow-up helps reinforce the strength of the relationship that was established during the process of conflict engagement and resolution. In addition, it provides a springboard for how you each individually and both together can handle future conflicts. You're building a foundation for recognizing what you do well in conflicts and what you need to work on.

> We believe that people are at their best when they work together to create opportunities for shared learning and growth. And that belief includes you.

This is the full cycle of the approach that implements a provisional response. You create a collaborative intentional plan, put it into action, and reflect on what happens. And you keep the wheel rolling, never falling for the fiction that you've solved all problems forever, always maintaining a healthy skepticism about any response's perfection, and collaborating all the way.

Share

Finally, we urge you and your collaborator to share what you've experienced and learned. In our decades of work leading programs, we have come to believe that nothing is more powerful than seeing two people who were stuck in seemingly intractable conflict come out the other side. Admitting the problem exists, describing how they've addressed it, working toward a more thoughtful, compassionate working relationship: when you show other people in your program, including staff, parents, and especially children, what you did and how you did it, you are modeling a way of approaching conflict that is profoundly meaningful.

You've Got This!

We hope you now see why we couldn't present a list of potential solutions to conflicts. It's not only that it's impossible to list them all—we've tried and failed. We also think that such lists are deceptive. The contours of every situation, the nuances of every relationship, have endless ramifications for each conflict, and ignoring those details to "solve" a problem is quick-fixing at its worst.

There's a final reason that we end by emphasizing the skills, understanding, and mindset we've discussed throughout the book. We believe in you! Both of us are profoundly constructivist educators: we believe that people are at their best when they work together to create opportunities for shared learning and growth. And that belief includes you.

We've written this book as a collaboration with you, one that mirrors the collaboration with others that's essential for finding your way through conflict. We have done our best to build a relationship with you, one that values the dynamic qualities of conflict. We've fronted trust, showing you our own foibles and follies. We've asked you lots of questions, knowing that you have answers that we do not. We've modeled the attitudes we hope you'll share.

Most importantly, we have invested confidence in you every step of the way. We believe that, despite your own foibles and follies, you have exactly what you need to find your way through conflict. We don't merely trust the process that this book describes. We trust that *you—and only you—have what it takes to make this process work for you.*

We sincerely hope that you can cultivate that confidence in yourself to find your way through conflict. It's a life journey with rewards on each step of the path.

Acknowledgments

From Both of Us

The central theme of this book is the importance of collaborating through difficulty, and the book would not exist without a remarkable network of peers, colleagues, and organizations over many years. To those we fail to remember in this acknowledgment, please know that we are deeply grateful despite our failure.

Many organizations have invited us to present this material for early childhood educators, including the annual conferences for the National Association for the Education of Young Children (NAEYC), Zero to Three, HighScope Educational Research Foundation, and the Educare Learning Network. We are grateful to the conference organizers who saw value in this work, and we are similarly grateful to the hundreds of participants who put their trust in us for two or three or six valuable hours. Over and over, working with individuals and groups to explore the contours and nuances of conflict, we succeeded and failed forward with them. This book would have been inconceivable without those people's willingness, vulnerability, and compassion. Their eager participation, feedback, and questions made us realize that this was truly important work for early childhood educators, and their anecdotes and insights suffuse this book.

As we started our work together on conflict, we spent several hours discussing the subject with an expert: Amy Gallo, editor at *Harvard Business Review* and author of the excellent *HBR Guide to Dealing with Conflict*. Her perspective, largely developed in the corporate sector, helped us clarify what we should and should not emphasize in the remarkably social world of early childhood education. More importantly, her affable, self-deprecating humor about this difficult work helped us make a temperamental shift that can be felt, we hope, in the tone of every page.

Many other smart people have written skillfully about topics we attempt to address in this book, including Sheila Heen, Patrick Lencioni, Bruce Patton, Kim Scott, Douglas Stone, and David Stroh. We hope we've done justice to their contributions with ours.

Ann McLain Terrell has demonstrated critical leadership for decades in early childhood education. We are deeply honored for her kind words in the foreword, and hope we can demonstrate her commitment to this work as the book takes life in the world. If nothing else, we aim to model that graceful leadership as best we can.

We are deeply grateful to the remarkable team at Free Spirit Publishing for supporting our hopes for this book, recognizing the need in the field, and responding with care and respect to every nit we picked. Judy Galbraith and Meg Bratsch have been cheering us on from the very start. Shannon Pourciau's design matched our own before we knew what it was. Amanda Shofner provided excellent marketing and publication support, and Alyssa Lochner's precise eye made us smile with control-freak glee every time she spied a copyediting error.

We are not the first, and won't be the last, authors who fail to find sufficient words to thank our editor and friend, Kyra Ostendorf. The books she has brought into the field of early childhood education are classics, and they take pride of place on our personal and professional bookshelves. When we learned that she would be joining the team at Free Spirit and thus available to work with us on our book, we were overjoyed.

Kyra met our hard-headed approach to what was right for this book with her equally hard-headed commitment to that vision, and her experience, intelligence, and skill made a better book than we could have imagined. We can't remember a single time when her insights didn't rightfully triumph over our confusion or ignorance. This book is immeasurably better thanks to Kyra, and we are immeasurably ennobled by our collaboration with her. We thank her from the bottom of our hearts.

From Chris

During the first week of October in 2015, I went to Washington, D.C., to chair the meeting of the Council for NAEYC Accreditation. We had three new members joining the Council that fall, and on the first day one of them, Christine Keena Snyder, immediately stood out. She was smart, poised, and had done all of her homework. Most impressively, she rightly called me out about a couple of items at her very first meeting. This, I thought, was someone I needed to know better.

By the time that trip to D.C. ended, we had started the conversation that would, first, launch a series of workshops and, then, lead to this book. Whenever I've been stuck in describing what someone should do and how someone should be in conflict, I just think of Christine and write what I know her to be. Her devotion to foundational principles in the field, her unapologetic commitment to equity, her precise teasing balanced by a keen self-deprecating humor, her refusal to back off the truth when it gets tricky, her deep respect and compassion for every human being: all of these inform the core components of the book. And they are what make her one of my most important, trusted friends. Thanks, CKS.

My wife, Andrea Castaneda, and our daughters, Bebe and Lulu, have been supportive, thoughtful, and forgiving family members during the months it took to write this book. Thankfully, we've generated reasonably few conflicts in that time—bad for the manuscript content, perhaps, but very good for its production. I love you all.

I've been lucky to find a professional home at the National Association for the Education of Young Children, and many colleagues with whom I've worked on various projects and committees inform this book as well, including Rhian Evans Allvin, Robyn Lopez Melton, Megan Madison, Tammy Mann, Ann Mitchell, Amy O'Leary, Gwen Simmons, Jerlean Daniel, and Barbara Willer. I apologize to the many remarkable colleagues whom I fail to mention here. And to every committee member with whom I've engaged conflict unskillfully: thanks for your kindness and forbearance. I'm still learning.

My colleagues at Tulsa Educare have patiently endured my verbose ramblings and lengthy emails about conflict, allowed me to test new ideas, activities, and formats, and have confronted me when some of those fall flat. I'm grateful to each one, but particularly to Cindee Bergren, Cindy Decker, Laura Fleming, Kelsey Horner, Nicole Kirkland, and Jennifer Ladner. I can't imagine better workmates.

Jane Gallop taught me how to read, write, and think with precision. 'Nuff said.

Though this is not a book about Zen Buddhism, so much of the content derives from the deepest principles of that practice: the inherent worth and awesome presence of every being, the value of turning toward difficulty, the intertwined reality of the relative and the absolute. I could not have found my way through the writing of this book without my teachers on this path, James Ford and Melissa Blacker, and those who have written so profoundly about how to walk it, most notably Norman Fischer and Diane Rizzetto. I offer 108 bows to each one of you.

Finally, Haven Miles taught me the central lesson of early childhood: the youngest children are complex, resilient, astounding human beings who deserve our care, compassion, and respect. When I began my career in early childhood education, she pointed me to key resources (especially Jack Shonkoff and the team at the Harvard Center for the Developing Child) and vibrant communities (the infant mental health and trauma-sensitive care communities in particular) without which I would have floundered far more often. In collaboration with her over many years at the Brown/Fox Point Early Childhood Education Center in Providence, RI, she taught me and many others how to see the world through a child's eyes, ears, nose, tongue, body, and mind.

Her sentences emerge regularly from my mouth. Her demand that we acknowledge and respect the rights of the littlest children fuels my drive. Her insights infuse this book in every way.

From Christine

First and foremost, my gratitude goes to my co-author, colleague, and friend, Chris Amirault, for his passionate engagement in our work together, belief in me when I have self-doubt, and genuine presence in all that he does. He is an endless fountain of wisdom and an essential figure in the early childhood education community. It is truly an honor to do this work together.

To my husband, Rob, and my children, Benjamin and Thomas, for their unwavering support of me and my relentless desire to say yes. Every time I commit to something new, they stand behind me with enthusiasm, confidence, and shared commitment. In the moments of my career when I felt most uncertain, defeated, and overwhelmed, they pushed me to keep going and never lost sight of the value of the work. All of my accomplishments are a reflection of the support and encouragement that I live with every day.

My career has been a collection of invaluable experiences with some of the best in the field. My mentors at Gretchen's House Child Development Centers raised me as a young teacher and taught me about growth and leadership, especially Heidi McFadden, Nan Farley, and Beth MeLampy. My colleagues at HighScope Educational Research Foundation taught me about resolving conflict with children, developed my ability to facilitate adult learners through difficult topics, and pushed me as a writer, especially Shelley Nemeth, Beth Marshall, Betsy Evans, Shannon Lockhart, Sue Gainsley, and Ann Epstein. A heartfelt thank you for the ongoing support of my passion and work beyond my day-to-day roles from my colleagues at the University of Michigan Health System Children's Center and Madonna University. I am indebted to all of you for the immeasurable space you have made for me to grow and thrive as a professional.

To the endless number of professional colleagues, family members, and friends that let me make mistakes and try again: The most valuable lessons I've learned came from moments when I was wrong and was afforded the opportunity to develop my perspective, consider the needs of others, and engage again. My commitment to the early childhood field and conflict engagement has everything to do with the people who supported me and worked with me through difficulty. This work is not an arrogant display of skill but rather a humble nod to the lessons I've learned through your grace.

Finally, my gratitude to the early childhood professionals who commit their life's work to supporting our littlest learners in their most vulnerable years. Without you, our work would be meaningless.

References

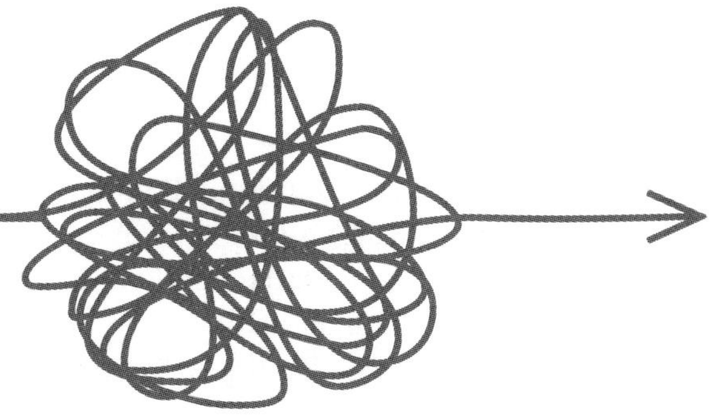

Bailey, Becky. 2015. *Conscious Discipline: Building Resilient Classrooms.* Oviedo, FL: Loving Guidance, Inc.

Bright Horizons Family Solutions, Inc. n.d. "Company Profile, Information, Business Description, History, Background Information on Bright Horizons Family Solutions, Inc." Accessed April 1, 2020. referenceforbusiness.com/history2/97/Bright-Horizons -Family-Solutions-Inc.html.

Elbow, Peter. 1998. *Writing Without Teachers.* 2nd edition. Oxford, UK: Oxford University Press.

Frei, Frances. 2018. "How to Build (and Rebuild) Trust." Filmed April 2018 for TED. ted.com/talks/frances_frei_how_to_build_and_rebuild_trust.

Gallo, Amy. 2017. *HBR Guide to Dealing with Conflict.* Brighton, MA: Harvard Business Review Press.

Goddard School. n.d. "What Makes us Different." Accessed April 1, 2020. goddardschool.com/philosophy/what-makes-us-different.

Goleman, Daniel. 2005. *Emotional Intelligence: Why It Can Matter More than IQ.* New York: Bantam.

Gretchen's House Child Care Centers. 2019. "Family Handbook." Revised June 2019. gretchenshouse.com/wp-content/uploads/2019/12/Family-Handbook-2018-NAEYC.pdf.

Hamilton, Diane Musho. 2015. "Calming Your Brain During Conflict." *Harvard Business Review.* December 22, 2015. hbr.org/2015/12/calming-your-brain-during-conflict.

Heshmat, Shahram. 2015. "What Is Confirmation Bias?" *Psychology Today.* April 23, 2015. psychologytoday.com/us/blog/science-choice/201504/what-is-confirmation-bias.

Kabat-Zinn, Jon. 1994. *Wherever You Go, There You Are: Mindfulness Meditation in Everyday Life.* New York: Hyperion.

Miller, William R., and Stephen Rollnick. 2012. *Motivational Interviewing: Helping People Change.* 3rd edition. New York: The Guilford Press.

Murray, Desiree W., Katie D. Rosanbalm, and Christina Christopoulos. 2016. *Self-Regulation and Toxic Stress: Implications for Program and Practice*. OPRE Report #2016–97. Washington, DC: Office of Planning, Research and Evaluation, Administration for Children and Families, US Department of Health and Human Services. fpg.unc.edu/sites/fpg.unc.edu/files /resources/reports-and-policy-briefs/SelfRegulationReport4.pdf.

National Association for the Education of Young Children. 2011. "Code of Ethical Conduct and Statement of Commitment." NAEYC position paper. naeyc.org/sites/default/files /globally-shared/downloads/PDFs/resources/position-statements/Ethics%20Position%20 Statement2011_09202013update.pdf.

Resnick, Brian. 2018. "The 'Marshmallow Test' Said Patience Was a Key to Success. A New Replication Tells Us S'more." Vox. June 6, 2018. vox.com /science-and-health/2018/6/6/17413000/marshmallow-test-replication-mischel-psychology.

———. 2019. "Intellectual Humility: The Importance of Knowing You Might Be Wrong." Vox. January 4, 2019. vox.com/science-and-health/2019/1/4/17989224 /intellectual-humility-explained-psychology-replication.

Rosanbalm, Katie D., and Desiree W. Murray. 2017. *Caregiver Co-regulation Across Development: A Practice Brief*. OPRE Brief #2017–80. Washington, DC: Office of Planning, Research, and Evaluation, Administration for Children and Families, US. Department of Health and Human Services. acf.hhs.gov/sites/default/files/opre/final_coreg _brief_10_22_2017_508_compliant.pdf.

Stone, Douglas, Bruce Patton, and Sheila Heen. 1999. *Difficult Conversations: How to Discuss What Matters Most*. New York: Penguin Putnam.

Stroh, David Peter. 2015. *Systems Thinking for Social Change: A Practical Guide to Solving Complex Problems, Avoiding Unintended Consequences, and Achieving Lasting Results*. White River Junction, VT: Chelsea Green Publishing Co.

Index

About the Authors

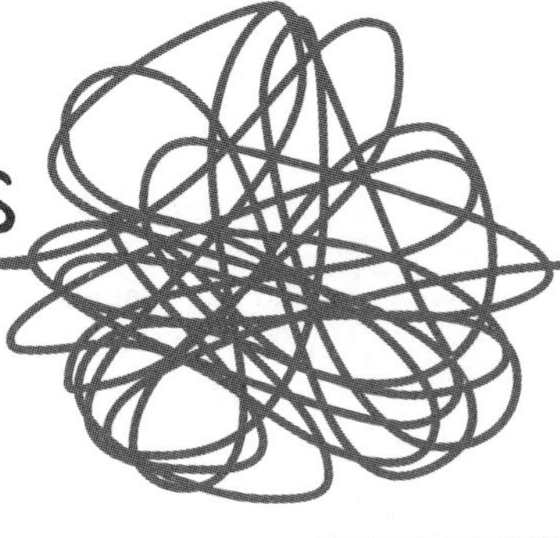

Chris Amirault, Ph.D., is the school director of Tulsa Educare MacArthur in Oklahoma, and for more than three decades has dedicated himself to high-quality education, teaching courses and facilitating workshops on early childhood education, conflict, assessment and instruction, ethics and professionalism, challenging behavior, family engagement, anti-bias education, and equity. Prior to his arrival in Tulsa, he lived in Mexico, working as a consultant focusing on organizational culture, change management, and QRIS system design in Oregon, Rhode Island, and California.

For thirteen years prior to that, he served as executive director of the Brown/Fox Point Early Childhood Education Center affiliated with Brown University in Rhode Island. During that time, he also taught early childhood education and development courses for area colleges and universities and served as a mentor and coach for providers throughout the community.

Chris also has an active volunteer life at the local, state, and national level. He served as the president of the Rhode Island Association for the Education of Young Children for several years, served as the chair of the Council for NAEYC Accreditation, and was a founding facilitator of NAEYC's Diversity & Equity Interest Forum. He lives in Tulsa, Oklahoma.

Christine M. Snyder, M.A., has worked in the early childhood education field since 1999 as a teacher, center director, author, and trainer/coach. She holds a master's degree in early childhood education and a bachelor's degree in child development. She is currently director of the University of Michigan Health System Children's Center and assistant professor in the college of education at Madonna University in Livonia, Michigan.

Previously, she was an early childhood specialist at the HighScope Educational Research Foundation in Ypsilanti, Michigan, where she focused on developing professional learning for teachers and curriculum for preschoolers and infants/toddlers. She facilitates training throughout the United States, internationally, and online, and has published several books, articles, training DVDs, and other classroom resources for teachers. She lives in Michigan.

Other Great Resources from Free Spirit

Uncover the Roots of Challenging Behavior
Create Responsive Environments Where Young Children Thrive
by Michelle Salcedo, M.Ed.
For early childhood educators.
192 pp.; PB; 8½" x 11"; includes digital content.
Free PLC / Book Study Guide
freespirit.com / PLC

A Moving Child Is a Learning Child
How the Body Teaches the Brain to Think (Birth to Age 7)
by Gill Connell and Cheryl McCarthy
For teachers, caregivers, special education practitioners, clinicians, and parents of children ages birth to 7.
336 pp.; PB; full-color; photos; 7¼" x 9¼"; includes digital content.

Mindful Classrooms™
Daily 5-Minute Practices to Support Social-Emotional Learning (PreK to Grade 5)
by James Butler, M.Ed.
For educators, grades preK–5.
192 pp.; PB; full-color; photos; 8½" x 11"; includes digital content.

Move, Play, and Learn with Smart Steps
Sequenced Activities to Build the Body and the Brain (Birth to Age 7)
by Gill Connell, Wendy Pirie, M.H.Sc., and Cheryl McCarthy
For early childhood teachers, caregivers, program directors, coaches, mentors, professional development trainers, and parents of children ages birth to 7.
216 pp.; PB; full-color; photos; 8½" x 11"; includes digital content.

Intentional Teaching in Early Childhood
Ignite Your Passion for Learning and Improve Outcomes for Young Children
by Sandra Heidemann, M.S., Beth Menninga, M.A.Ed., and Claire Chang, M.A.
Presented in partnership with Redleaf Press
For early childhood teachers and providers, instructional coaches, directors, and administrators.
216 pp.; PB; 7¼" x 9¼"; includes digital content.
Free PLC / Book Study Guide
freespirit.com / PLC

For pricing information, to place an order, or to request a free catalog, contact:

Free Spirit Publishing Inc.
6325 Sandburg Road, Suite 100
Minneapolis, MN 55427-3674

toll-free 800.735.7323 • local 612.338.2068
fax 612.337.5050

help4kids@freespirit.com • freespirit.com